MILL

NORTH AMERICA

Boston
Providence
New York City

EUROPE

ENGLAND

FRANCE

Acknowledgments

This book would have been far more difficult to write and significantly less complete without the advice and expertise of several people. For their interest and generosity I would like to thank the following:

Patrick M. Malone at the Slater Mill Historic Site, who withstood seven readings of the manuscript.

Theodore Z. Penn of Old Sturbridge Village, particularly for his help on power transmission.

Thomas Leary, for his patience.

John Chaney, for his first-hand knowledge of the nineteenth century.

Myron Stachiw, Charles Parrott, Jack Lozier, Helena Wright, Betsy Bahr, Sarah Gleason, Richard Greenwood, Elizabeth Sholes, Jeff Howry, and Ruth Macaulay, to whom, for her editorial assistance and extraordinary tolerance, this book is lovingly dedicated.

V   10   9   8   7   6   5   4   3

Library of Congress Cataloging in Publication Data

Macaulay, David.
  Mill.

  1. Textile factories—Rhode Island—History. I. Title.
TS1324.R4M33   1983   677'.009745   83-10652
ISBN 0-395-34830-7

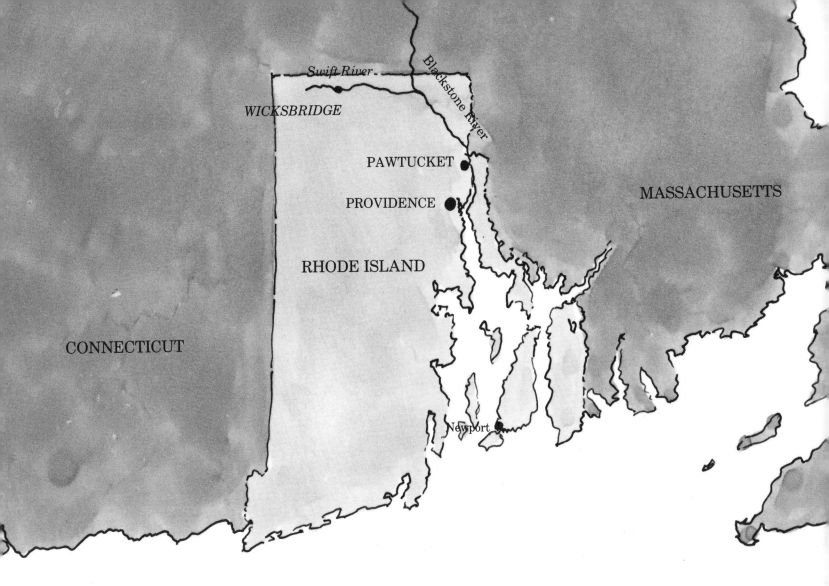

PREFACE

The mills of Wicksbridge are imaginary, but their planning, construction, and operation are typical of those developed throughout New England during the nineteenth century.

Each New England mill is an architectural statement of the financial resources and ambitions of its owners. The permanence and often remarkable state of preservation of these mills are a tribute to the ingenuity and hard work of their builders. The number and density of communities that grew up around the mills still recall the lure of financial independence and personal prosperity that these structures once symbolized. In their physical domination of the surrounding landscape, however, many mills continue to remind us that no opportunity comes without a price.

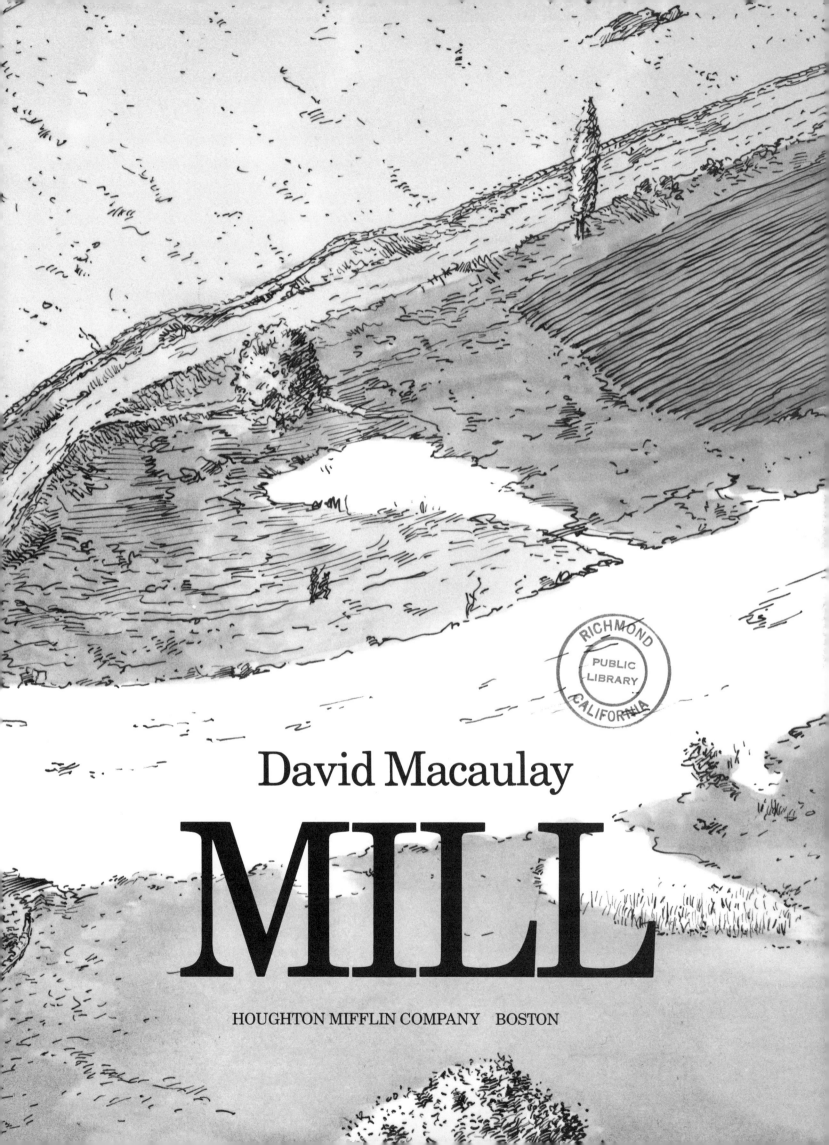

David Macaulay

MILL

HOUGHTON MIFFLIN COMPANY   BOSTON

INTRODUCTION

Cotton must first be spun into yarn before it can be woven into cloth. For centuries this was done by hand in the home. After being cleaned and prepared, the individual fibers were carefully drawn and twisted into a continuous thin strand and wound around a spindle. The spun yarn was then transferred to looms, on which it was woven into fabric.

The mechanization of spinning and weaving, which resulted in the creation of the textile industry, was part of an unprecedented period of technological invention known as the Industrial Revolution. It began in England in the middle of the eighteenth century and continued well into the nineteenth century in Europe and the United States.

A new kind of building was designed to house great numbers of these new machines so they could all be run from a central power source. Long, narrow, multi-storied structures, some using water wheels, others steam engines, were built in both England and Scotland. They were called either manufactories or mills.

These mills spawned an increase in production that brought with it the need to find new markets and to protect old ones. As the prime exporter of textiles to Europe and North America, Great Britain jealously guarded any new developments in either machinery or manufacture that might encourage others to compete. A shortage of technical expertise along with an abundant supply of imported cloth did little to encourage the development of America's own textile industry.

However, in the fourth quarter of the eighteenth century things began to change. Not only did the United States win political independence, but a growing number of Americans wanted greater economic independence. British immigrants familiar with the textile industry were welcomed along with their knowledge, and by 1793 a recent arrival named Samuel Slater had built and was operating America's first successful cotton spinning mill in Pawtucket, Rhode Island, using the water power of the Blackstone River.

While spinning cotton with water-powered machinery was unknown in America before the 1790s, the use of water power for a variety of other tasks had been well established. Almost every New England river and stream of any size had at least one mill, usually more.

WHEELPIT

TAILRACE

   By 1800, a saw mill, a fulling mill, and a grist mill, all powered by water wheels, stood near a waterfall on the Swift River, a tributary of the Blackstone fifteen miles north of Pawtucket. Each wheel turned in its own stone-lined enclosure called a wheelpit, and each wheelpit was linked to the river by a channel called a raceway. The portion of the raceway that delivered water to the wheel was called the head-race; the portion that returned it to the river after it had turned the wheel was called the tailrace.

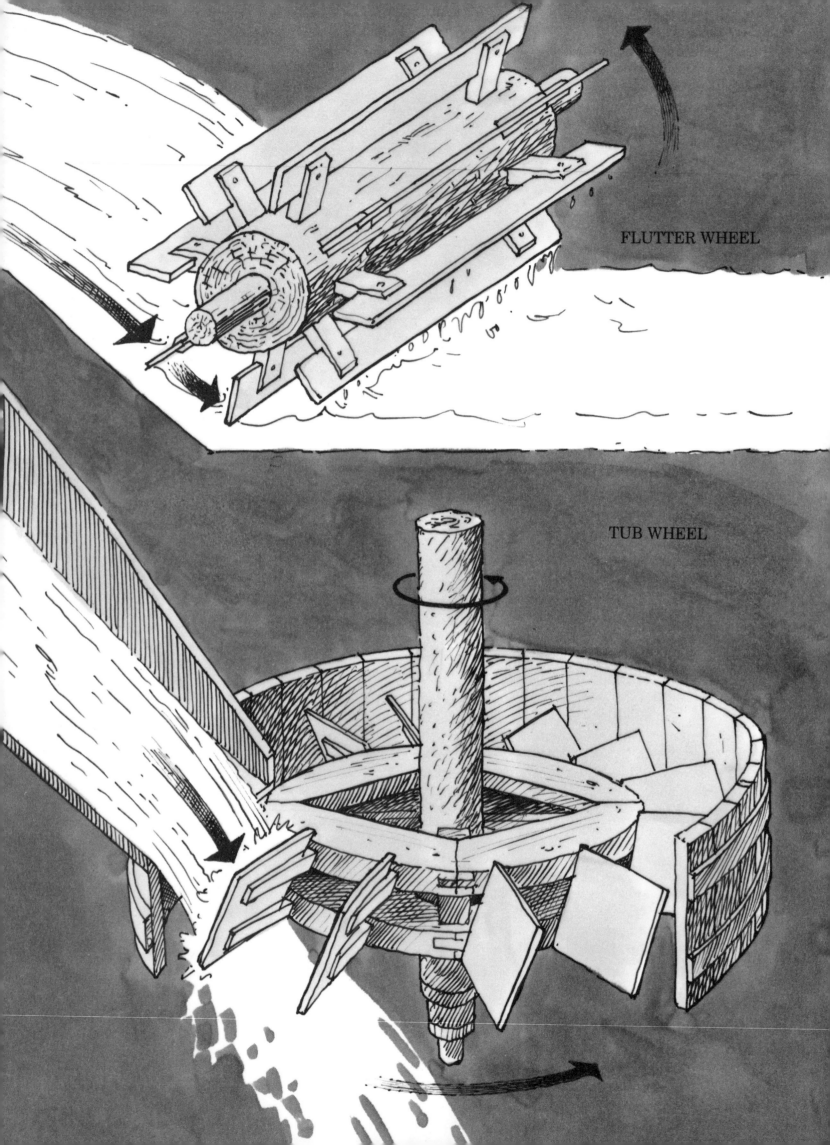

FLUTTER WHEEL

TUB WHEEL

The saw mill contained two water wheels. The first, called a flutter wheel, operated the up-and-down saw while driving the log into the blade. The flutter wheel was basically a horizontal shaft from which radiated a number of boards called blades. It turned as the water passing underneath it pushed the blades.

The second wheel was a tub wheel. It powered the machinery that withdrew the log once it had been cut. It, too, was turned by the force of the water against its blades. In this case, however, the blades were attached to a vertical shaft and enclosed by a round wooden tub.

In the fulling mill, woolen cloth woven by local families was pounded by wooden hammers to clean and thicken it. The hammers were powered by an undershot wheel. Although much larger than the flutter wheel, it was also turned by the force of the water flowing under it and striking its blades.

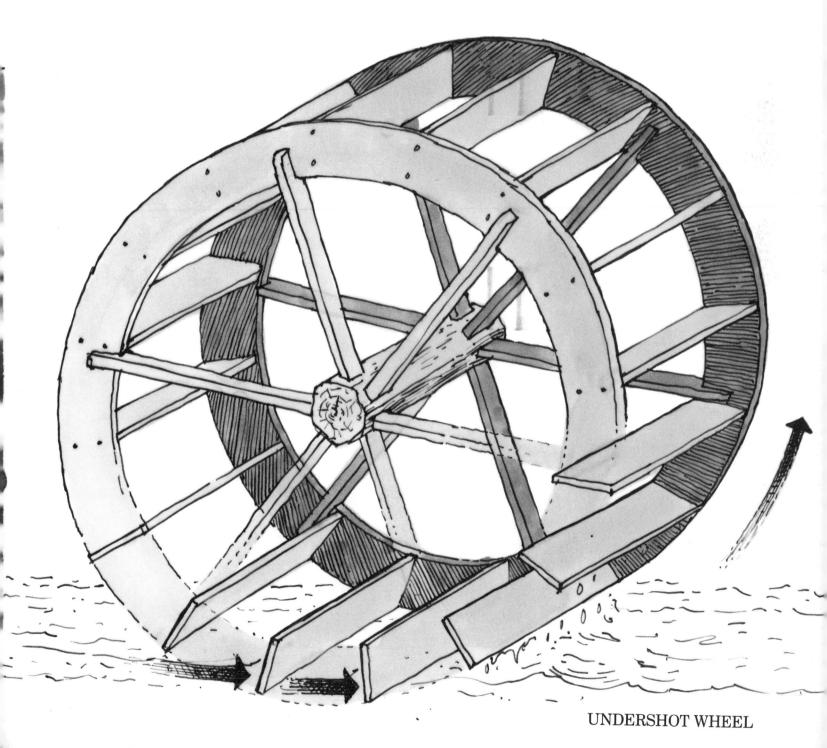

UNDERSHOT WHEEL

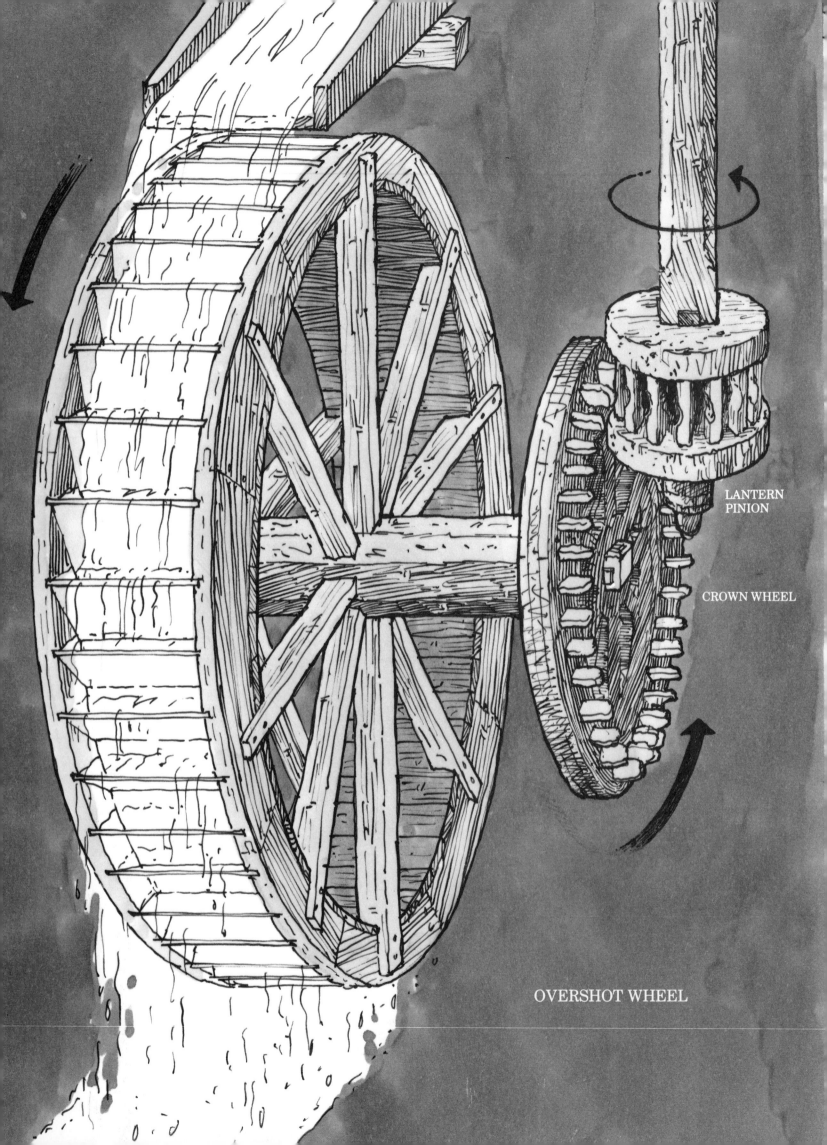

LANTERN
PINION

CROWN WHEEL

OVERSHOT WHEEL

The grist mill ground corn and wheat for many of the area's farmers. It was powered by a large overshot wheel. Instead of having blades, the perimeter of the overshot wheel was constructed with a continuous row of wooden troughs called buckets. Water from the headrace poured over the top of the wheel and into the buckets. The weight of the water in the buckets turned the wheel.

The vertical distance the water drops between headrace and tailrace is called the head. The amount of power available at any site was dependent on both the head and the rate of flow.

When the equipment in a mill couldn't be run directly from the shaft of the water wheel, a system of gears, additional shafts, pulleys, and belts called a power train was required. In the grist mill, the shaft of the wheel extended beyond the wheelpit and into the space below the first floor. A flat wooden wheel called a crown wheel was attached to this extension. A circle of wooden cogs projected from one side of the crown wheel near its rim. They meshed with and turned a cylindrical, wooden, cage-like structure called a lantern pinion. This gear revolved on a vertical shaft that was connected through two additional gears and a smaller shaft to the upper millstone. Because the diameter of the lantern pinion was only one quarter that of the circle of cogs, it turned four times for each revolution of the crown wheel. By going from larger to smaller gears in this way the millstone could be turned over a hundred times every minute while the water wheel turned only seven.

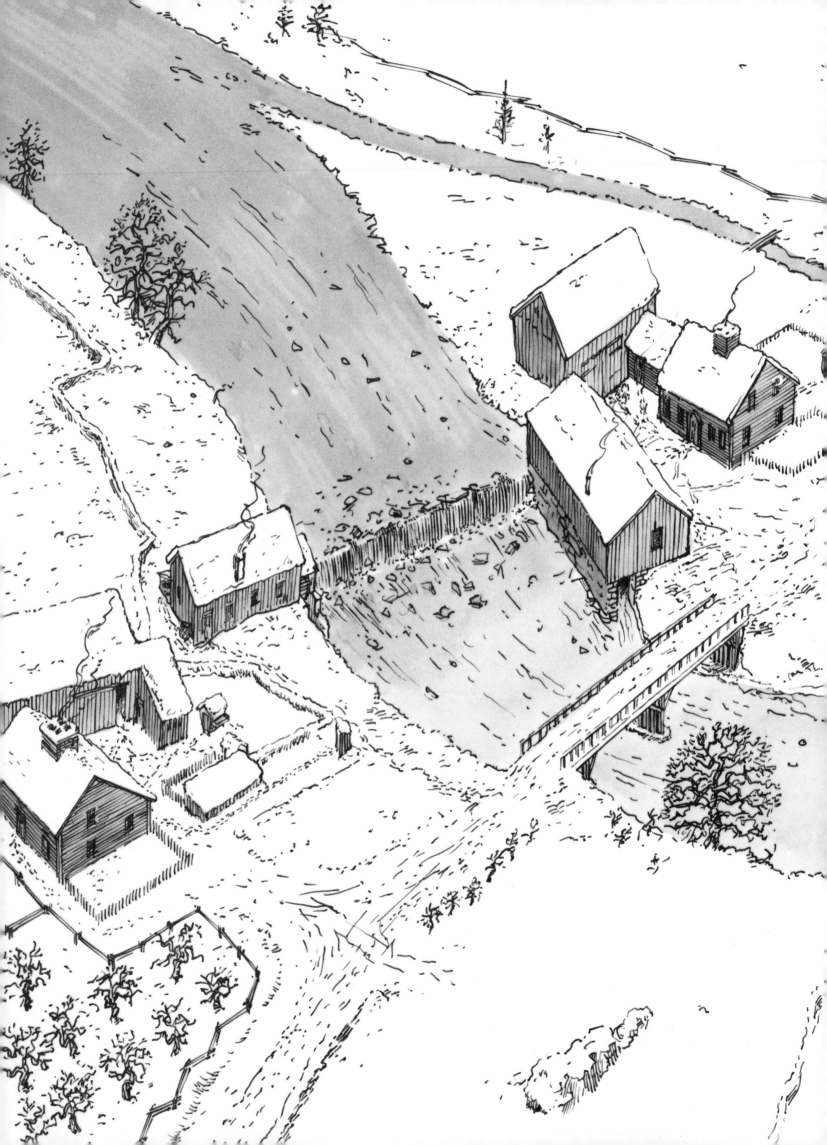

Existing water power technology, the periodic arrival of new technical information and expertise, and the desire for economic independence combined to turn the production of cloth into a growing if not immediately profitable business. Perhaps the greatest boost to this fledgling enterprise came unintentionally, near the turn of the century, from Europe.

While Great Britain was determined to maintain its economic dominance over the Continent by monopolizing that market for so many of its manufactured goods, France, under Napoleon, was attempting to establish a unified and economically independent Europe. Both countries, therefore, forbade any neutral country to trade freely with the other. Since all of Europe was basically at war, the only neutral country seriously involved in foreign trade was America, and its ships were harassed and seized by both the British and the French. The United States responded in 1807 by prohibiting the importation of any foreign goods. By 1809 the embargo applied only to British and French goods and by 1810 only to British goods. Although generally opposed by merchants and considered an absolute disaster by those in the shipping industry, this series of restrictions forced investors to find other uses for their money. One of the most prominent beneficiaries was the American textile industry.

THE YELLOW MILL

On February 27, 1810, a partnership was formed in Providence, Rhode Island, for the purpose of building and operating a cotton mill. The older partners, who knew almost nothing about setting up such a mill, included Silas Wicks, Zenus and Sylvanus Chaney, and Judge Pardon Fiske. Wicks and the Chaney brothers had amassed considerable fortunes in shipping and foreign trade; Fiske's wealth came from farming. The youngest partner, twenty-seven-year-old Zachariah Plimpton, had grown up in England and knew a great deal about cotton textile manufacture. At the age of fourteen, he had been apprenticed to a prosperous mill owner and for the next eight years had worked in every area of cotton spinning, weaving, and factory management. He came to America at the age of twenty-two to escape an arranged marriage and soon found work as an agent, managing a small Rhode Island mill. The subsequent success of that mill established Plimpton's reputation as one of the ablest men in the business.

At their first meeting, each partner took responsibility for a particular aspect of the new venture. Wicks and Judge Fiske would pay for the machinery and initial supply of cotton. The Chaneys were to provide the materials, workers, and money to build the mill. Plimpton was to design and supervise the construction of the mill and to act as its agent when it was finished. At his suggestion, the partners agreed to operate about seven hundred and fifty spindles for spinning cotton and to run all the machinery with water power.

Plimpton soon compiled a list of available mill sites, and on Monday, March 19, he set off to choose the best one. The requirements that concerned him most were access to a river for power and to a road or canal for transportation. At each location he first estimated the river's flow, and determined the highest available head.

ONE QUARTER MILE

THREE HUNDRED YARDS

WATER FALL

10 ft

RAPIDS

3 ft

5 ft

PROFILE OF THE SWIFT RIVER

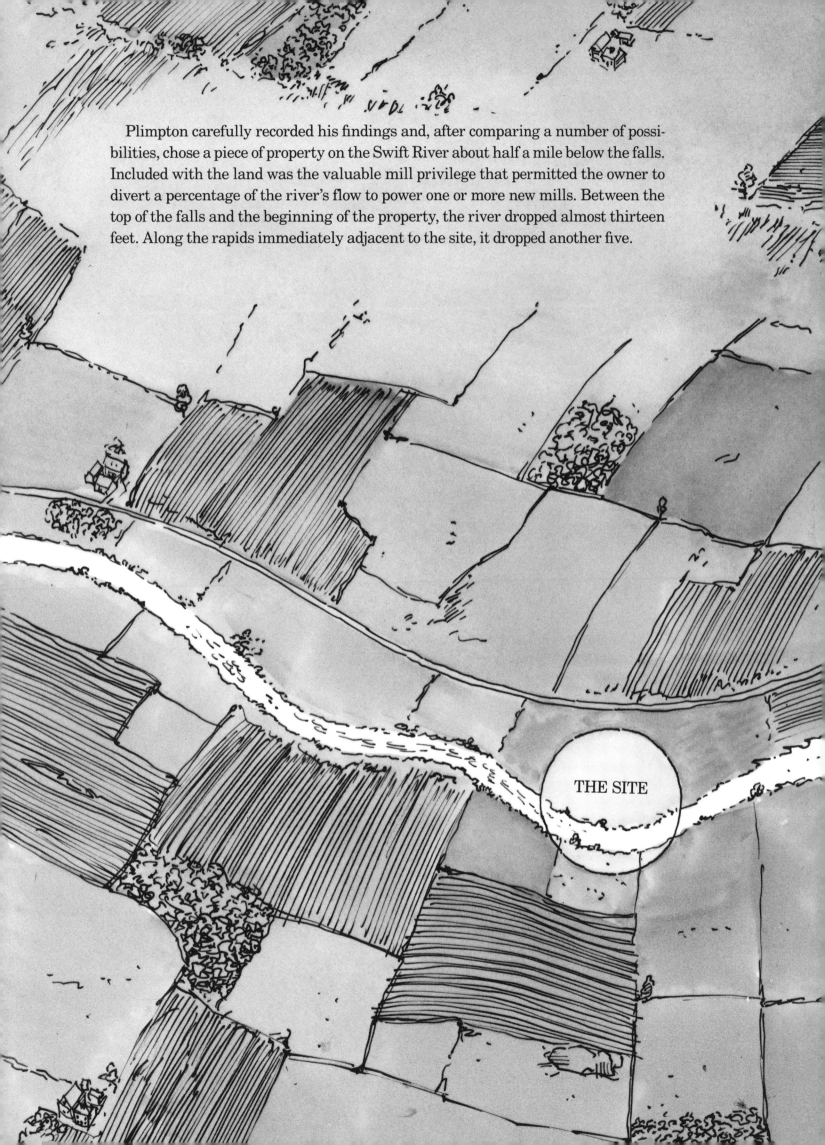

Plimpton carefully recorded his findings and, after comparing a number of possibilities, chose a piece of property on the Swift River about half a mile below the falls. Included with the land was the valuable mill privilege that permitted the owner to divert a percentage of the river's flow to power one or more new mills. Between the top of the falls and the beginning of the property, the river dropped almost thirteen feet. Along the rapids immediately adjacent to the site, it dropped another five.

THE SITE

COMPARISON OF WHEELS IN BACKWATER

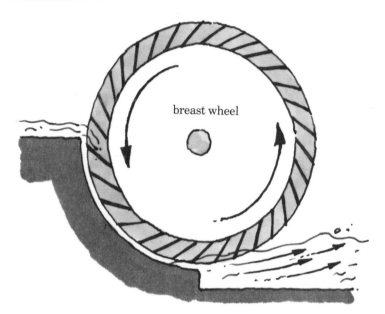

breast wheel

overshot wheel

On his return to Providence, Plimpton set about designing a water wheel that would use the river's power most efficiently. He calculated that by building a dam across the rapids he could create a six- or seven-foot head without affecting the mills upstream. After comparing the power from each type of wheel with the needs of the machinery, he settled on a breast wheel. Like the overshot wheel, it was turned by the weight of the water in its buckets, but it did not require as great a head. Instead of coming over the top of the wheel, water entered the buckets of the breast wheel from the upstream side and turned in a direction opposite to that of the overshot wheel. Plimpton saw this as a great advantage in times of flooding. The higher the water level in the river, the more chance there was of it backing up into the wheelpit and decreasing the efficiency of the wheel. Because of its direction of rotation, the breast wheel would tend to push the backwater away, whereas the overshot wheel would draw it underneath itself and further reduce its efficiency.

The floor of the wheelpit on the upstream side was carefully formed to follow the circumference of the breast wheel. This curved section of floor, called the breast, left so little space between itself and the wheel that the water was kept in the buckets until they had reached the lowest point in their rotation. Because water entered the buckets midway up the height of the wheel, the wheel Plimpton designed was called a midbreast wheel.

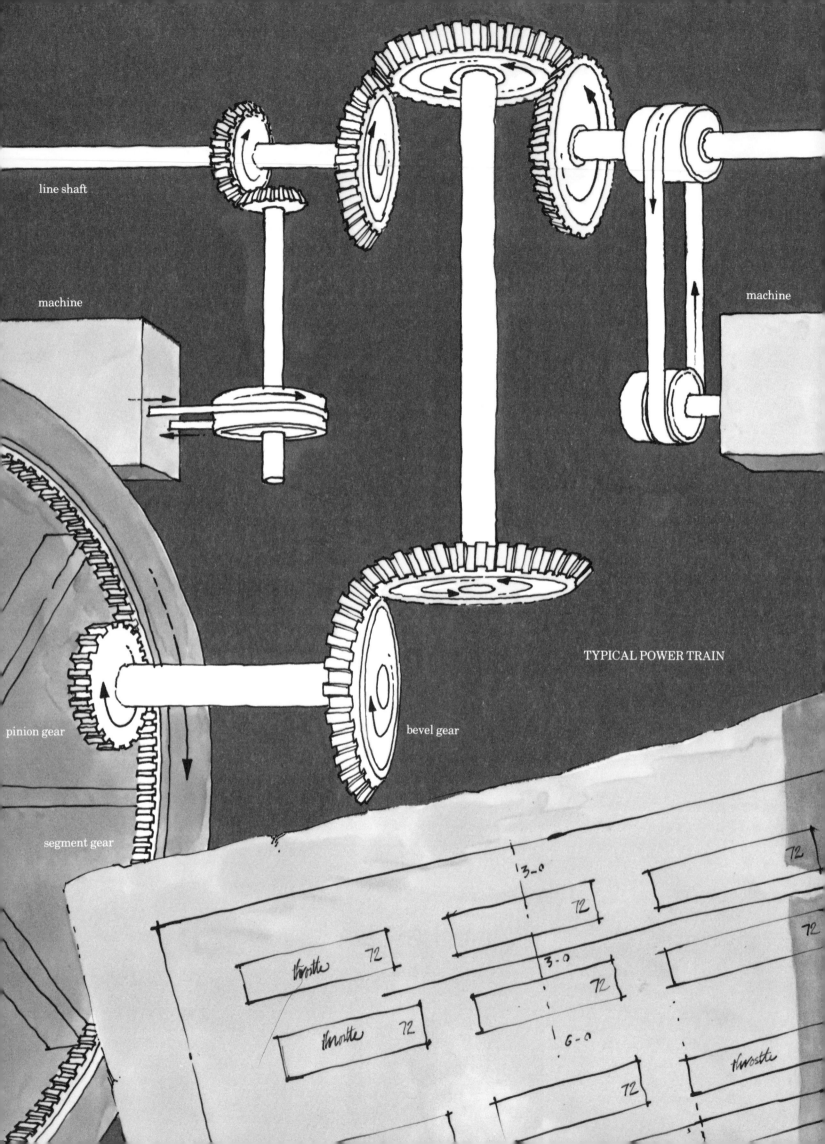

line shaft

machine

machine

pinion gear

bevel gear

segment gear

TYPICAL POWER TRAIN

Although he could plan the mill based on the amount of machinery it had to house, Plimpton could not determine its precise dimensions without first designing the power train. The rotary motion of the water wheel was transferred to a vertical shaft through an arrangement of bevel gears. Through an additional set of bevel gears, the rotation of the vertical shaft was transferred to a horizontal shaft called a line shaft. Each machine was connected to the line shaft either by a small vertical drive shaft or by a continuous rope or leather belt.

After determining the length of the longest line shaft, Plimpton decided on the length of the building. The width was established by first laying out the machinery along the line shafts and then placing the walls as close to it as possible, in order to let the most daylight into the work space.

Because of its availability, wood was the most practical building material. Since most of his experience in England had been with brick and stone construction, Plimpton hired a millwright named Benjamin Quigg to design the building's timber frame and to supervise its eventual construction.

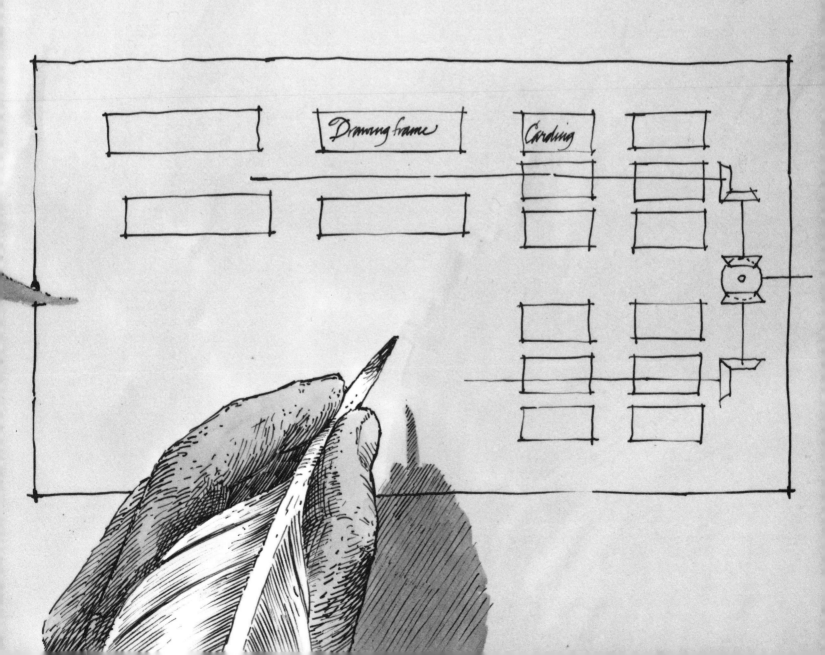

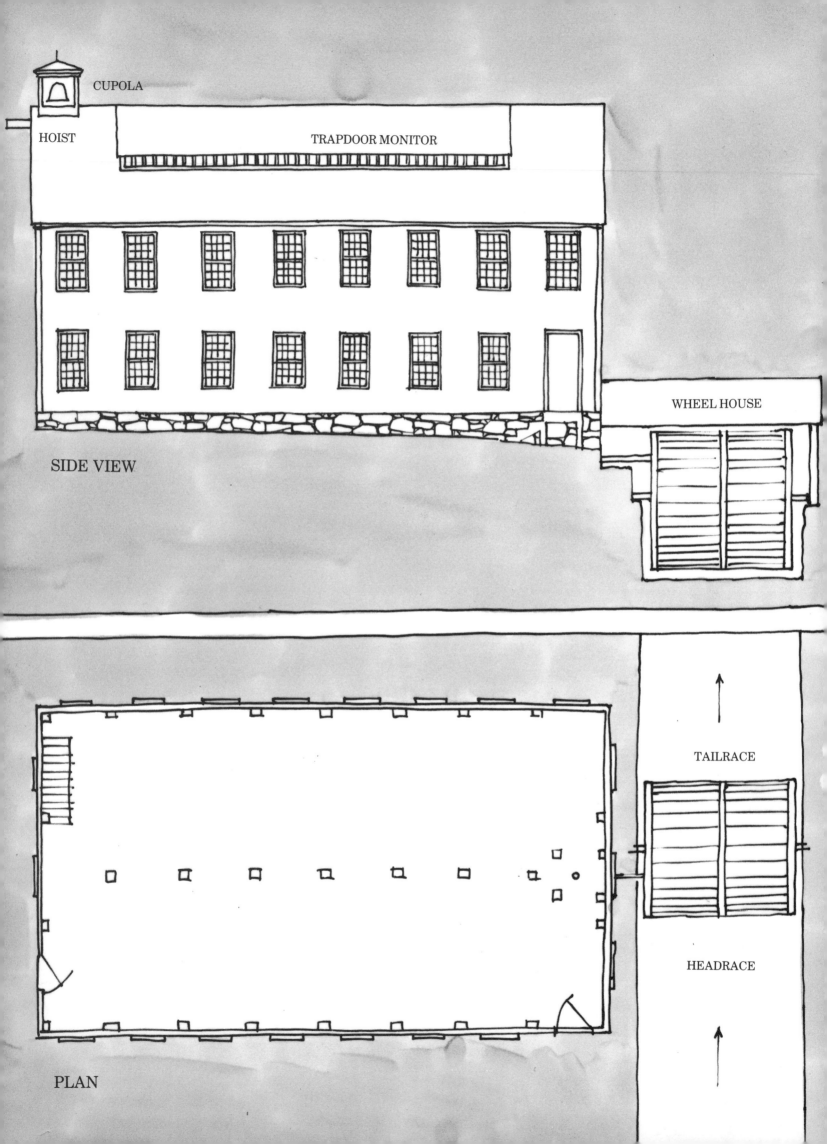

CUPOLA

HOIST

TRAPDOOR MONITOR

WHEEL HOUSE

SIDE VIEW

TAILRACE

HEADRACE

PLAN

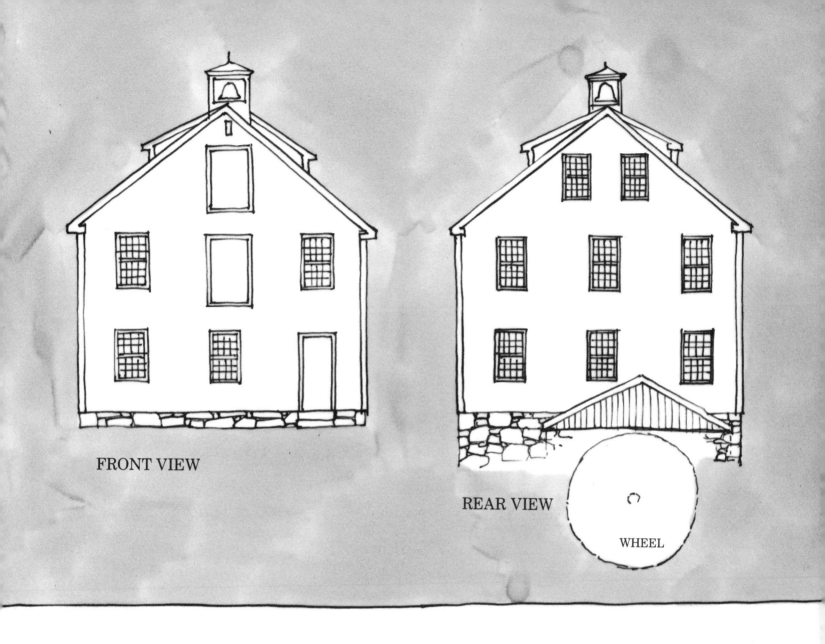

FRONT VIEW

REAR VIEW

WHEEL

In early April, Plimpton presented the plans to his partners. The mill was to be sixty-four feet long by thirty-four feet wide, with two full stories and a usable attic. While comparatively large windows would serve the lower floors, two narrow strips of windows, called trapdoor monitors, one on each side of the roof, would let light into the attic. At one end of the building, he had placed a small projecting shed to house the wheel. On the peak of the roof at the other end, he had designed a simple cupola to house the bell.

They were all delighted with Plimpton's efforts and urged that construction begin as soon as possible.

After calculating approximately how much timber would be needed for the siding, roofing, and flooring, Quigg went to a number of saw mills near the site and bought all the well-seasoned wood he could find. Plimpton remained behind to order such items as window frames, glass, nails, tools, and various cast-iron pieces, which were to be manufactured in the Providence area.

Two days later, Plimpton joined Quigg at the Eagle, a tavern near the falls. Both men rented beds there for the duration of the project.

The following morning, Quigg began felling trees he had already marked for the main frame of the building. Plimpton, meanwhile, made arrangements with a local farmer to quarry stone for the foundations and wheelpit from an exposed ledge on his property.

Two weeks later, close to a dozen men, most of them itinerant laborers lodging at nearby farms, were quarrying stone and loading it onto sleds.

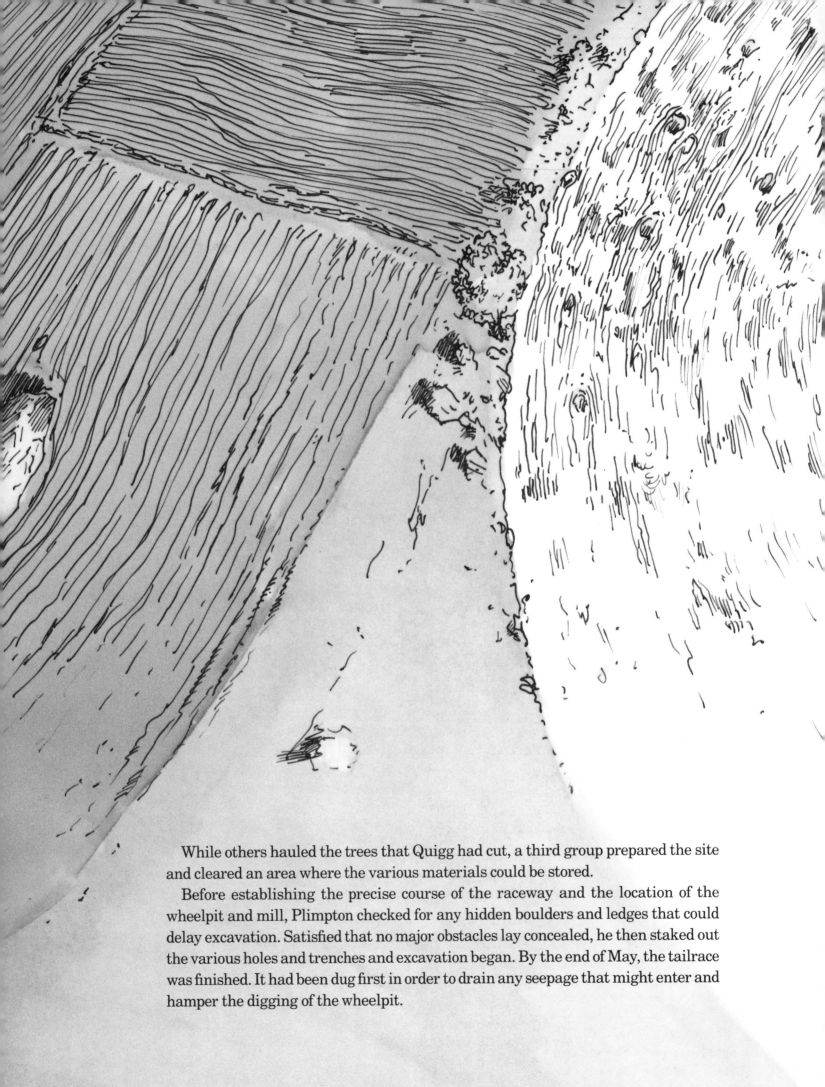

While others hauled the trees that Quigg had cut, a third group prepared the site and cleared an area where the various materials could be stored.

Before establishing the precise course of the raceway and the location of the wheelpit and mill, Plimpton checked for any hidden boulders and ledges that could delay excavation. Satisfied that no major obstacles lay concealed, he then staked out the various holes and trenches and excavation began. By the end of May, the tailrace was finished. It had been dug first in order to drain any seepage that might enter and hamper the digging of the wheelpit.

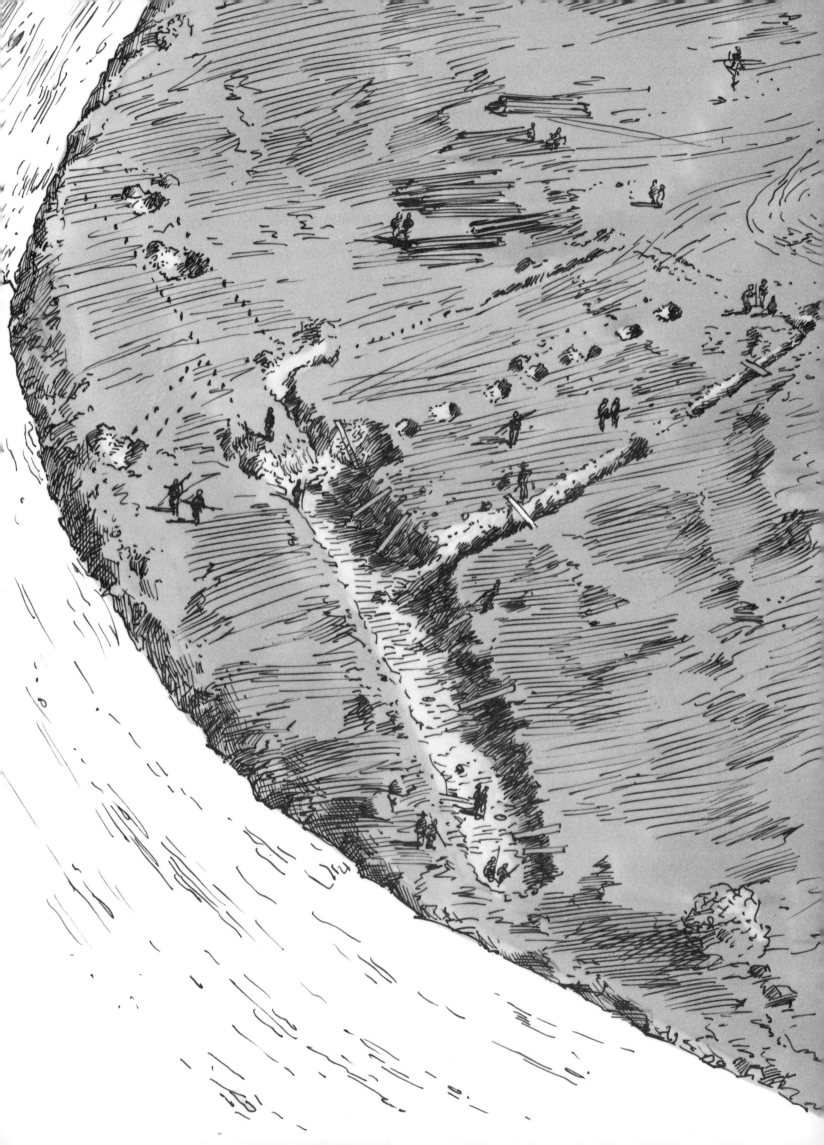

Plimpton lined the bottom of the wheelpit with a wooden floor, to speed the departing water by reducing friction and to prevent the water from washing out the soil under the side walls. The breast was then secured to the floor and to the walls. After setting each curved timber rib into place Quigg tied them together with a layer of thick planks. The space inside the breast was filled with rock and gravel. Before Quigg nailed down the last plank, Plimpton indulged his superstitions and slipped a coin behind the face of the breast for good luck. It was a Roman coin he had discovered in England when digging his first wheelpit.

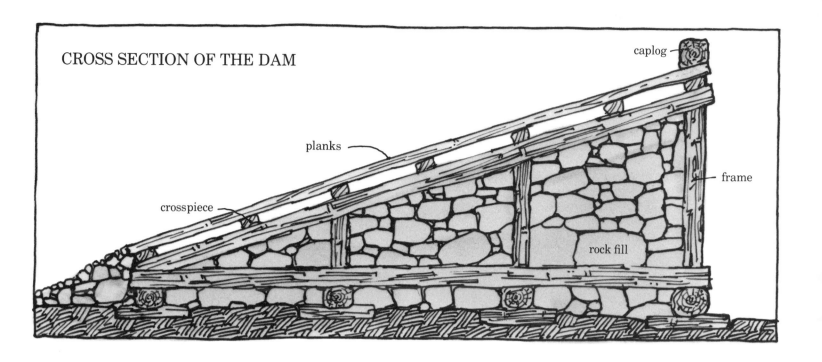

CROSS SECTION OF THE DAM

caplog

planks

frame

crosspiece

rock fill

In early August, when the level of the river was at its lowest, Quigg turned his attention to the construction of the dam. It would consist of two identical wooden ramps projecting slightly upstream from stone abutments on each bank. The two would cross the lower rapids and meet in the center. Each ramp would reach a height of six feet and taper back about twenty-five feet. Workers assembled the pieces of the framework on the banks, but before they could be moved into place the riverbed had to be drained. This was done a section at a time, using a temporary dam called a coffer dam. It extended from the bank to about the center of the river and consisted of large wooden baskets dragged into position and sunk with rocks. Clay was packed between them to seal the barrier further.

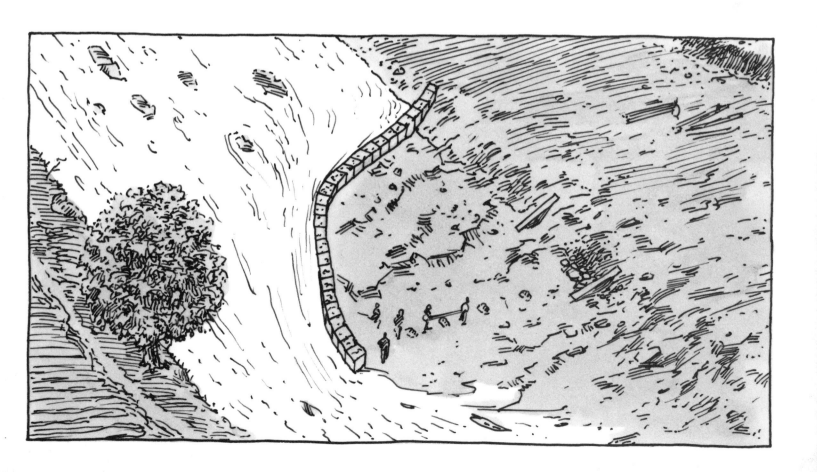

When the water below the coffer dam had drained away, the loose rock and rubble were cleared and a number of heavy timbers were set into trenches cut in the river-bed and pinned in place with iron rods. The frames were then secured to the timbers and connected by crosspieces. After filling the space inside the frame with rocks, Quigg covered the dam with a layer of planks. The combined weight of the water and the rocks would hold the dam in place. On the top or crest of the dam, Quigg secured a caplog to reduce wear on the ends of the planking. When the first half of the dam was completed, the coffer dam was removed and the process repeated on the other side of the river.

While the dam was under construction, much of the headrace had been dug and lined. Several feet of embankment at the entrance to the headrace were not excavated, to prevent water from entering the channel until all work in the wheelpit had been finished.

From a point in the headrace near the wheelpit, Plimpton dug a smaller channel called a spillway. It would be used to drain the headrace for repairs and as a safety precaution in times of flooding.

By September the stonework was complete and most of the timber for the building had arrived. While the planks were being cut at the saw mill, Quigg and a few skilled assistants had hewn each post and beam to its required shape and size.

Many of the pieces were to be fastened together using a system of tenons and mortices. Tenons are projecting wooden tongues that are precisely cut to fit into matching slots called mortices. Each connection was then to be secured with a wooden dowel called a treenail. The tenons, mortices, and treenail holes were all cut or bored and checked for fit before assembly began.

On its completion, the foundation was capped with heavy beams called sills. Notched into the sills and spanning the width of the foundation was a row of parallel floor beams, the centers of which rested on stone piers. Smaller beams, called joists, connected the main beams and supported two layers of one-inch-thick floor planks.

The main structure of the building was to be a row of thirty-foot-wide parallel frames locked together by sturdy horizontal beams. The space between each frame, called the bay, measured roughly seven and a half feet. Starting at one end of the floor, the frames were assembled and then left lying approximately where they would stand.

On the evening of August 31, as the last pieces of the end frame were being fastened together, a mud-splattered coach pulled into the yard behind the Eagle. Plimpton was there to welcome Wicks and the two Chaneys, who had come to watch the raising of the frame the following day.

By the time Wicks and the Chaneys arrived at the site early the next morning, over a hundred and fifty men, women, and children from the surrounding farms had already gathered. While some farmers had refused to help build a factory in their rural area, others were only too pleased to help create a new market for their agricultural products and various skills.

As soon as the visitors were settled, Quigg gave the order to raise the first frame. This was done slowly and carefully using ropes and pulleys attached to a temporarily secured vertical timber called a gin pole. The tenons below each post were gently guided into their mortices in the sill. Once the frame stood straight, it was held in place while the frame adjacent to it was raised using both the gin pole and individually held poles called pikes. Both frames were then connected at the second-floor

level by two horizontal beams called girts and at the attic level by two more horizontal beams called plates. The plates were locked in place by beams that ran across the width of the mill and tied the end posts of each frame together. Diagonal bracing was used to secure the structure further. This process was repeated down the length of the building, and by late afternoon the entire skeleton stood assembled.

No sooner had the last peg been driven into place than the entire group broke into a loud, spontaneous cheer. Shortly thereafter a spirited party began, which didn't end until all the food and drink had been consumed. It was close to one in the morning before the last workers wandered back to their respective barns and farmhouses.

girt

trapdoor monitor

plate

vertical planking

clapboard siding

By the time Plimpton arrived at the site the following Monday morning, a portion of the structure had already been enclosed by heavy vertical planking and Quigg was clambering around, supervising the construction of the second floor.

When the attic floor was finished, pieces of the roof frame were hoisted onto it, assembled, and raised. When the entire frame was complete, it was covered by a layer of planking followed by a layer of overlapping wooden shingles. As each wall of vertical planking was completed, it was sealed by overlapping horizontal boards called clapboards and painted yellow.

The interior surface of the vertical planking was covered by narrow strips of wood called lath, to which a thick coat of plaster would be applied once the window frames had been installed.

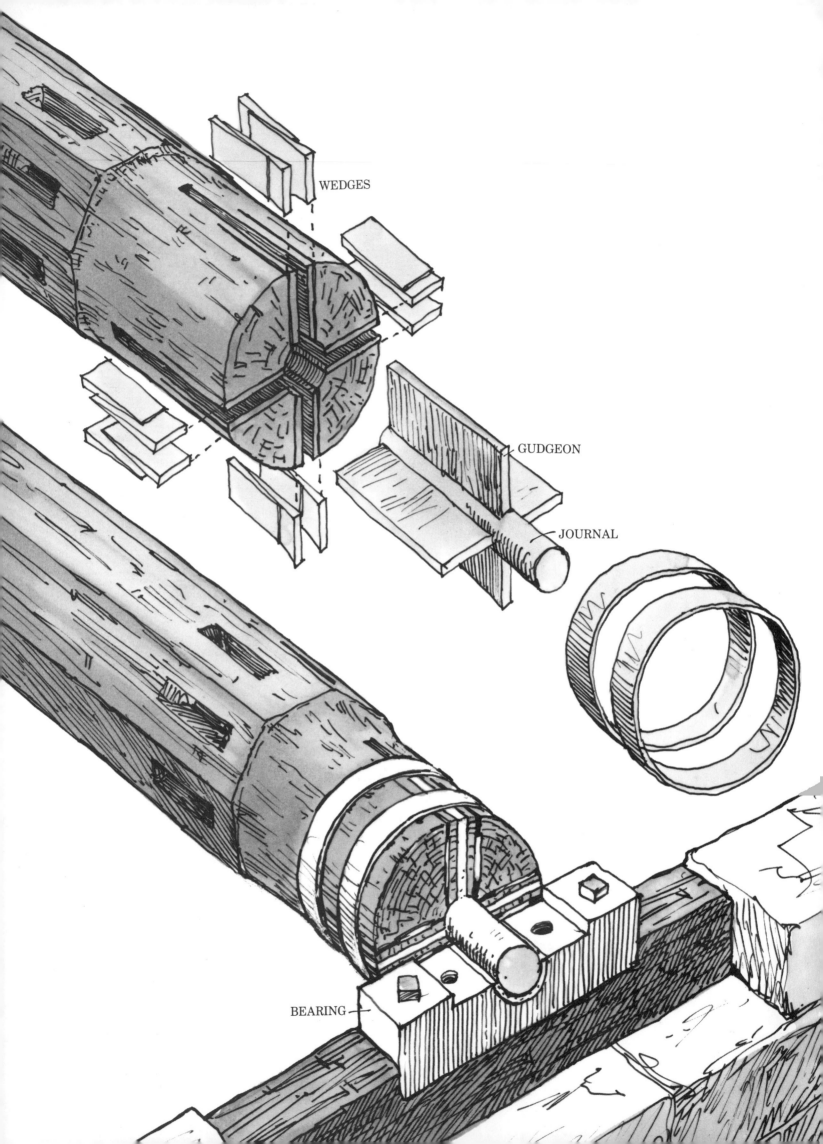

WEDGES

GUDGEON

JOURNAL

BEARING

SPOKES

BREAST

FELLOE

While Quigg had been supervising the construction of the building, Plimpton had been concentrating on the wheel. It had to fit into the pit as closely as possible, so the size and shape of each piece was double-checked before being cut. The heavy timber shaft that would carry the weight of the wheel was shaped first. The spokes were cut next and fitted into slots around each end of the shaft. Both rims of the wheel, comprised of thick segments called felloes, were then constructed to tie the ends of the spokes together. Plimpton had a series of carefully measured grooves cut into the inside faces of the felloes to receive the boards that would serve as the fronts of the buckets.

An iron extension called a gudgeon was wedged into grooves at each end of the shaft and secured by iron bands. The projecting cylindrical ends of the gudgeons, called journals, were to revolve in cast-iron bearings. Each bearing was lined with bronze to reduce friction and secured to one of the beams on each side of the wheelpit. Once the shaft had been set in place and leveled, workers inserted the spokes and secured the rims.

The space between the rims was then enclosed by a continuous barrel-like surface of planks called the soaling. The soaling not only tied the sides of the wheel together but also served as the back of each bucket.

The last pieces of the wheel to be assembled were the bucket faces. Before each board was slipped into its grooves, two small holes were drilled through each one and covered on the inside by leather flaps. These acted as valves, which would automatically close as water entered each bucket. They would open again as it left, preventing the formation of a vacuum in the bucket as it rose from the wheelpit. A vacuum would hamper the exit of the water and in turn retard the rotation of the wheel.

When the wheel was finished, the entire pit was enclosed by the wheel house.

Between the end of the headrace and the wheelpit, a pair of wooden gates was installed to control the amount of water entering the buckets and thus the speed of the wheel. A screen of closely spaced inclined wooden strips, called a trashrack, was placed across the headrace just in front of the gates to prevent debris that might damage the wheel or breast from entering the pit.

In early October, the upper end of the headrace was excavated and lined. Across the entrance, Plimpton floated a log called a trash boom. It was secured to both banks and protected the headrace from larger pieces of floating debris.

While the shafting for the power train was to be wood, the gears were to be cast iron. The first gear had already been installed in segments inside the rim of the water wheel closest to the building. Its teeth, which faced the horizontal wheel shaft, turned a smaller gear called a pinion.

The pinion was attached to a second horizontal shaft that extended into a space below the floor of the mill. At the opposite end of this shaft was a large vertical bevel gear. The teeth on its angled rim were designed to mesh with those on a horizontal bevel gear at the base of the vertical shaft.

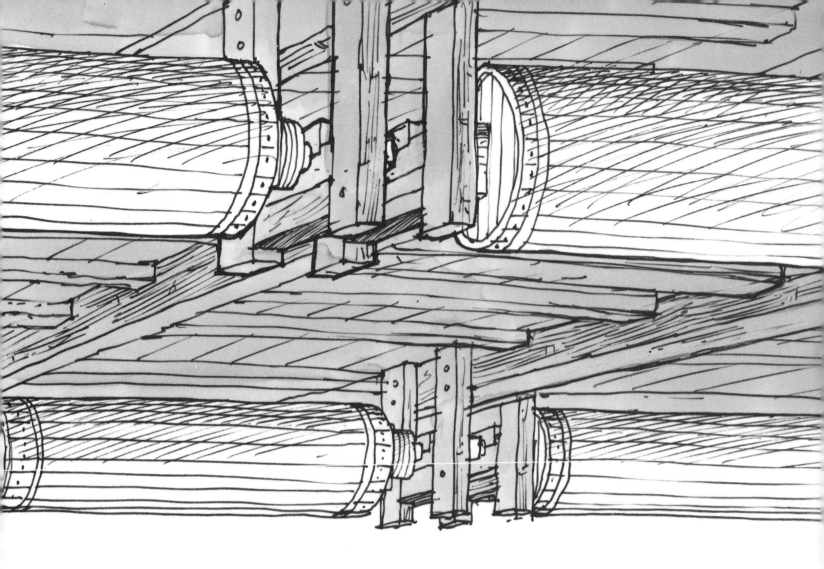

Both the vertical and horizontal shafts were built of sections fastened end to end. This made the shafting easier to install, and easier to repair. A square bar of iron was set into the end of each section of shaft. Two bars were then joined using a square cast-iron sleeve called a coupling. A journal was cut into each iron bar so they could rotate in their bearings.

At the wheel-house end of the mill, Quigg had built a sturdy timber frame from the first floor to the attic to support the vertical shaft of the power train and keep it in line.

Once the vertical shafting and its gears were in place, Plimpton suspended two line shafts from the ceiling above each of the main floors. Constructed around the sections of line shaft were narrow wooden drums over which the belting would revolve.

While the power train was under construction, the water wheel had been shut down. It was just before Thanksgiving when Plimpton raised the gates again. Slowly the wheel reached its operating speed and so did the power train. The mill shook slightly and was filled with a grinding rumble. Everyone put down their tools. A few of the more skeptical workers even left the building. But the vibrations gave Plimpton great satisfaction, and Quigg never doubted for a moment that his structure could withstand anything Zachariah might ask of it.

With the insertion of window glass, the installation of a number of cast-iron stoves, and the whitewashing of the interior wood and plaster, the building was finished. By December most of the pieces for the various machines had arrived, and they were assembled during the winter months.

All the machines Plimpton had purchased were equipped at one end of their horizontal drive shafts with two identical pulleys located side by side. One was fixed permanently to the shaft while the other turned freely around it.

Attached to each machine next to the pulleys was a lever called a belt shifter. The leather belt from one of the main line shafts, which would run continuously unless the water wheel was stopped, was first placed around the loose pulley. To turn a machine on, the operator simply pushed the lever that guided the belt off the loose pulley and onto the fixed or fast pulley.

When the first bales of cotton arrived that March, Plimpton had them delivered to a number of surrounding farms, where the cotton was cleaned by a process called picking. Although the seeds had been removed on the plantation by a machine called a cotton gin, the bales still contained twigs, leaves, insects, and dirt. The picking process involved placing the raw cotton on a wooden frame and beating it with a stick to release these impurities. The cleaned cotton was then returned to the mill, where it was mixed with clean cotton from other bales to produce a more homogeneous material.

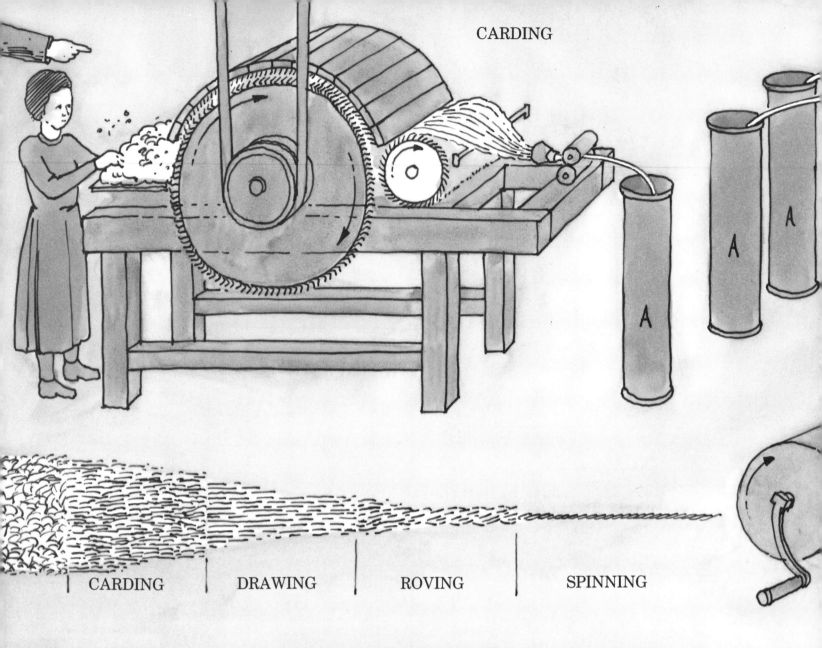

CARDING   DRAWING   ROVING   SPINNING

By April, most of the machinery was installed and, understandably, Plimpton was anxious to try it out. He first fed a quantity of mixed cotton into a carding machine, where it passed between opposing layers of wire teeth. In this machine, the cotton fibers were untangled and aligned. What emerged, with all its fibers more or less parallel, was a loosely connected rope called a sliver. Next, Plimpton carefully eased a number of slivers into a machine, by which they were drawn and combined into a single, stronger sliver. He repeated this drawing process a number of times. The finished sliver was then fed into a roving machine, where it was not only drawn further but, as it dropped into a revolving container called a roving can, was given a very slight twist. The roving, as the cotton was now called, was then removed from the roving can and wound around a bobbin.

When enough bobbins had been filled, they were taken upstairs to a spinning machine called a throstle. The throstle continued and refined the drawing process but performed a much stronger spinning and twisting action as it wound the finished yarn around another bobbin on one of its seventy-two spindles. The yarn on these bobbins was then tied into bundles called hanks, ready for delivery to one of the many weavers who would manufacture the cloth.

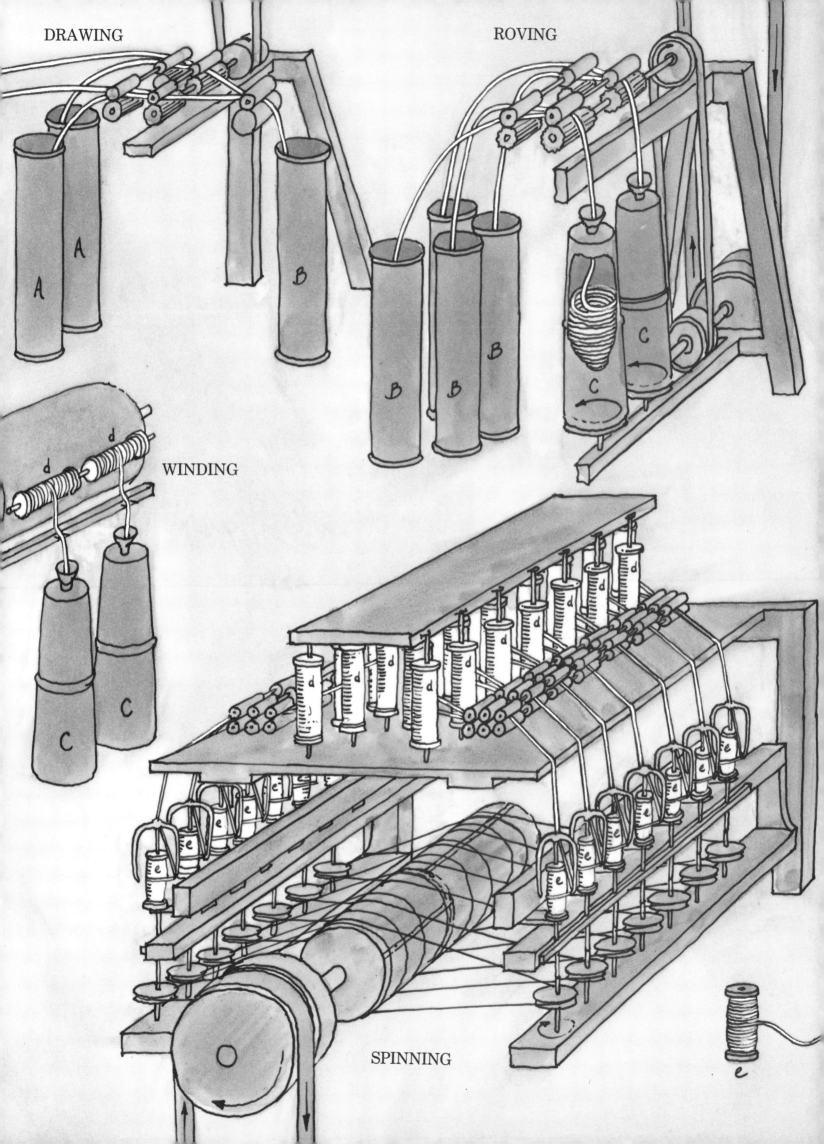

DRAWING

ROVING

A

A

A

B

B

B

B

B

B

C

C

WINDING

d

d

d

C

C

C

d

d

d

d

d

d

d

d

d

d

d

d

e

e

e

e

e

e

e

e

e

e

SPINNING

e

While Plimpton was assembling and testing the various machines, Quigg supervised the construction of a number of smaller buildings around the mill. These included a storage shed, closest to the mill, and, a little farther away, a privy. Between the mill and the main road, he built two identical wooden houses for the mill workers and a stone cottage for Plimpton.

By mid-April only a handful of workers remained on the site, and two of them asked for permanent employment in the mill. On April 29, Quigg and the other builders left to work on a new mill about six miles upstream.

On the following day a widow named Lucy Tripp arrived with her five children. They quickly moved their few belongings into one of the wooden houses. Plimpton had hired Mrs. Tripp to keep one of the houses and to take in two boarders, one of whom was Luther Daggett, who would oversee the spinning room. The Tripp children, ranging in age from six to thirteen, would all work in the mill.

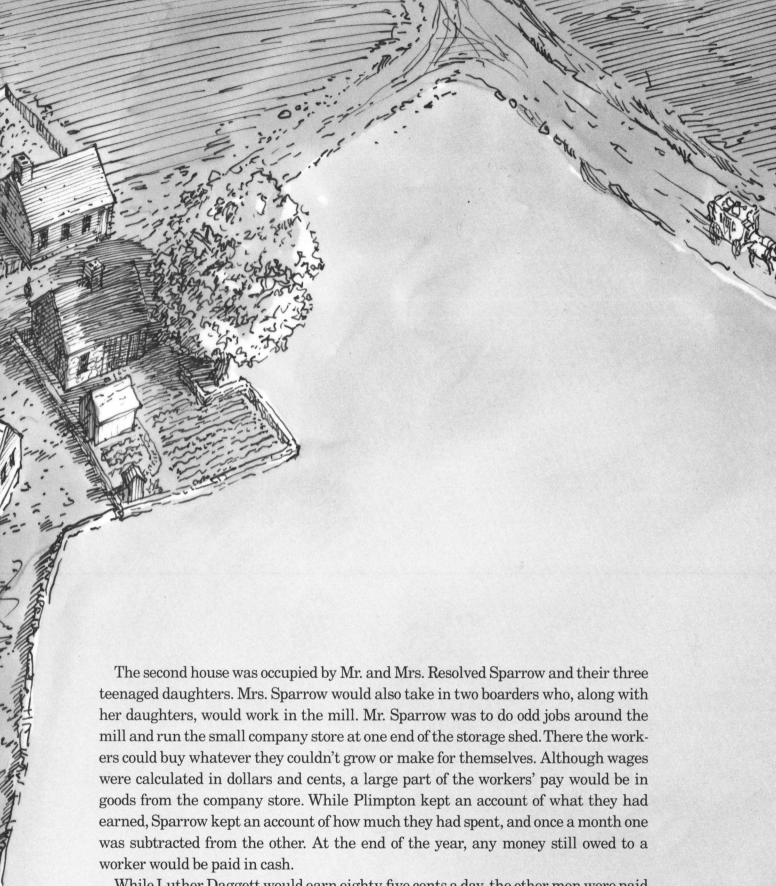

The second house was occupied by Mr. and Mrs. Resolved Sparrow and their three teenaged daughters. Mrs. Sparrow would also take in two boarders who, along with her daughters, would work in the mill. Mr. Sparrow was to do odd jobs around the mill and run the small company store at one end of the storage shed. There the workers could buy whatever they couldn't grow or make for themselves. Although wages were calculated in dollars and cents, a large part of the workers' pay would be in goods from the company store. While Plimpton kept an account of what they had earned, Sparrow kept an account of how much they had spent, and once a month one was subtracted from the other. At the end of the year, any money still owed to a worker would be paid in cash.

While Luther Daggett would earn eighty-five cents a day, the other men were paid closer to seventy-five cents. The women would earn around thirty-five cents a day and the children would average about fifteen cents. For their houses and accompanying small plots of land, Mrs. Tripp and the Sparrows paid the mill about twenty dollars a year. Mrs. Tripp also paid a nearby farmer twelve dollars a year for the care and feeding of the family cow.

On June 25, 1811, the first sacks of yarn were lowered onto Elisha Crawford's wagon. Crawford, who worked for a number of spinning mills, had been hired to distribute the finished yarn among various weavers, some of whom lived as far away as Connecticut. He would also return the finished fabric to the mill. After receiving Plimpton's approval, it would then be shipped to a cloth merchant in Providence.

Excerpts from the Diary of Zachariah Plimpton

1811	July 4	Independence Day. All hands out. Repaired and greased one of the throstles and wrote to my brother.
	July 5	Boys rang bell at 5 A.M., all hands left at 7 P.M.
1812	June 24	Miss Abigail Chaney and myself were united in holy wedlock this morning at nine-thirty at Providence.
	July 7	This war with England seems most unnecessary, though I expect it will increase the demand for our yarn.
1813	March 6	Gudgeon on vertical shaft broke again today. Have sent to foundry for replacement.
	July 6	Mrs. Plimpton and I are blessed with our first-born, a daughter. We have named her Mary for my mother.
1814	May 3	Ned Talbot agreed to clean off old grease and grease water wheel gudgeons, main gears, and machinery for twenty-five cents a week in addition to his regular wages.
	August 3	Our son William was born at quarter past three this morning. He and Mrs. P. in excellent health.
	December 30	Down to last cord of firewood, have ordered ten more from J. Spencer, who gave best price.
1815	April 10	Twelve-year-old Anna Tripp lost three fingers today feeding carding machine. Have instructed all the children to take more care.
	June 6	New picking machine is installed, will no longer have to send cotton out.
	August 17	We thank God for a second daughter, Ruth, born today.
	November 13	Three orders for our yarn have already been canceled this month. My old countrymen are ruining me with their great amount of cheap cloth, better we were at war again. I have heard of two mills closing already.
1817	March 27	Mr. Wicks and a number of his associates have been granted a charter to operate a turnpike. It will run close by and greatly ease transportation of our goods.
	October 22	We have named our second son Zachariah. Seems more frail than either his brother or sisters.
	December 25	Bell rung at 6 A.M. Spent two hours removing ice from wheel and gate. All machinery running by eight-thirty.
1818	September 1	Samuel, our third son, born today. The new house is almost ready, thank God!
	November 16	Sarah Tripp quit today, has gone to work at Boston Manufacturing Company in Waltham.
1819	January 11	God has taken our Zachariah after two weeks with croup. It was my sad duty to dig his small grave under the elm behind the house. Will order a stone from Fletchers.

Excerpts of a Letter from Selinda Sparrow to Her Sister in Pomfret, Connecticut

April 1819

My dear Prudence,

We were all pleased to hear the wonderful news and hope that the baby is well. I think Selinda is a perfect name for her and am most flattered. Things have not changed much around here since your departure. Poor Mr. and Mrs. Plimpton's little son died earlier this year. Mr. Plimpton was greatly shaken but seems a little better now. The mill helps take his mind from the sorrow, I think. Mrs. Plimpton is fortunately distracted by the other children ... Sarah Tripp has written from Waltham and asked after you. She is now operating three looms and making over a dollar for every hundred yards of cloth. I cannot hope to earn so much here and often think of joining her there ... But she also complains of the noise in the weaving room. Although it is not quiet in our mill, I think it must be more so than at Waltham. My ankles no longer swell as often as they once did, and the illness Mother told you about seems to have passed ... Ned, who now works in the machine shop, has begun calling upon me.

Excerpts from the Diary of Zachariah Plimpton

1820	April	15	Today the partners undertook to spin only coarse yarn, to be woven into "Negro cloth" with which the gentlemen from the southern plantations can clothe their slaves.
1823	March	15	Have installed two power looms on third floor, will run them off the second floor line shaft.
1825	August	19	The meetinghouse was struck by lightning last night and burned to the ground.
	September	24	With a generous donation from Mr. Wicks, we were able to raise the frame of the new meetinghouse today.
	September	25	We held a service under the new frame this morning.
1827	September	30	Tremendous gales all night. Saw mill and fulling mill badly damaged. River burst its banks and took bridge.
	October	4	Mr. Wicks is planning to build us a fine stone bridge. Have to travel five miles at present to cross the river.
1828	August	14	New bridge is most impressive. Some are now referring to our little community as Wicksbridge. Mr. W. seems quite pleased.
	September	30	Completion of Blackstone Canal only three miles away has further eased our transportation problems.
	November	14	Mr. W. has suffered a blow of fortune. Shipping losses in the Orient have forced him to sell his shares in the Yellow Mill. Mr. Sylvanus Chaney and myself have offered to purchase them.
1829	May	22	Mr. Zenus Chaney died earlier this week of lung fever.
	June	6	Mr. Sylvanus C. informed me today that he has inherited all his brother's shares. My father-in-law and I are now sole partners in the Yellow Mill.

THE STONE MILL

A depression in 1829 drove many textile mills out of business. In order to survive, Zachariah Plimpton had been forced to cut production at the Yellow Mill, but by the autumn of 1830, things had changed drastically and he could no longer keep up with the demand. As the number of slaves working the southern plantations continued to grow, the production of "Negro cloth" became increasingly profitable. At the urging of Waldo Ripley, a cloth merchant and friend of the Chaney family in New York, Zachariah and Sylvanus decided in October to build a new mill that would weave as well as spin. It would contain two thousand spindles, sixty-six power looms, and all the equipment necessary to run them.

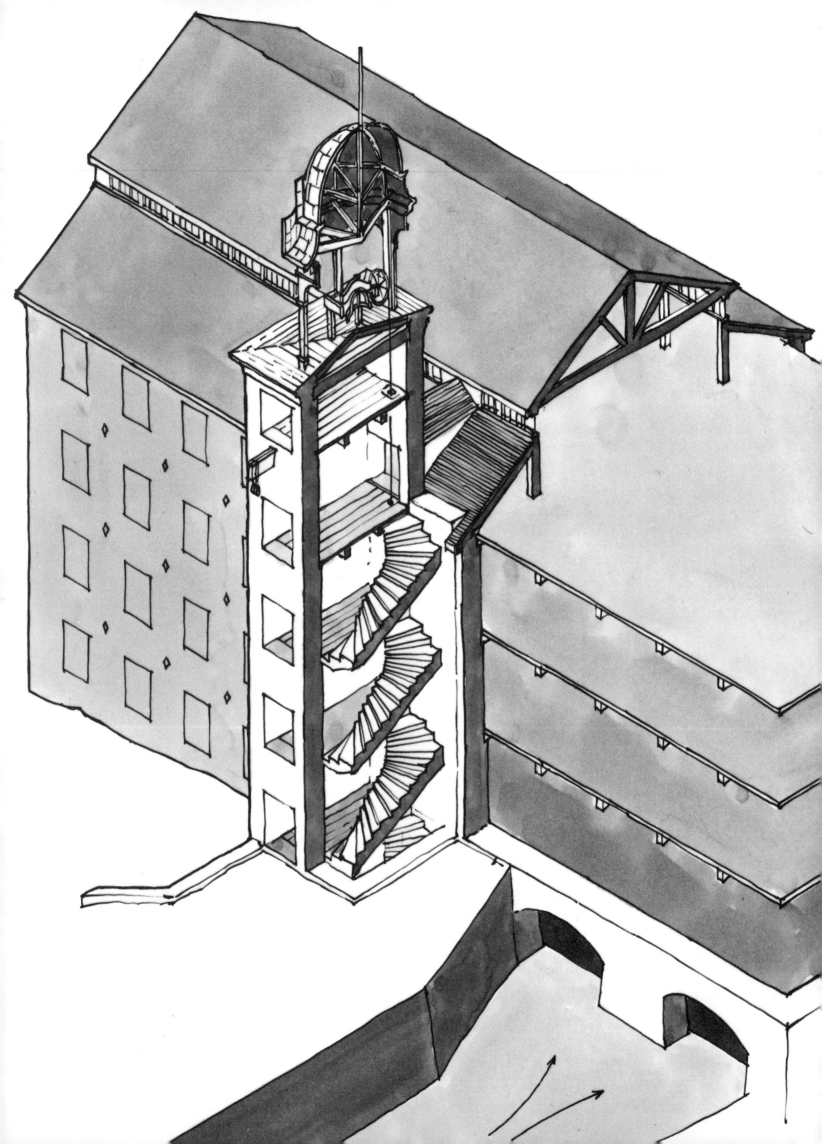

Once the machinery had been laid out, plans were drawn up for a stone building one hundred feet long by forty-five feet wide. It would contain three floors, a basement, and a large attic. To obtain maximum floor space for the machinery and to reduce the possibility of fire spreading from one floor to another, the stairs were to be enclosed in a large stone tower projecting from the front of the mill. It would also contain a loading platform for each of the floors. To save the time lost traveling to an outdoor privy, a toilet for each floor was placed in a wooden tower attached to the rear of the building. Chutes from each of the toilets would empty directly into the tailrace.

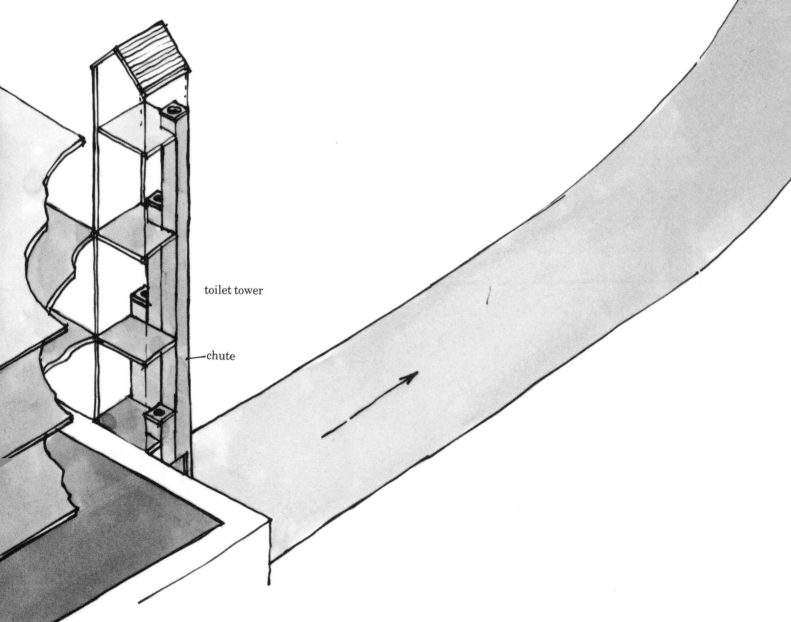

toilet tower

chute

While larger windows would again let in light for the three main floors, the attic was to be served by the smaller windows of a clerestory monitor. The monitor was the raised uppermost section of the roof; the clerestory was the two spaces between the monitor and the lower, outer sections of roof.

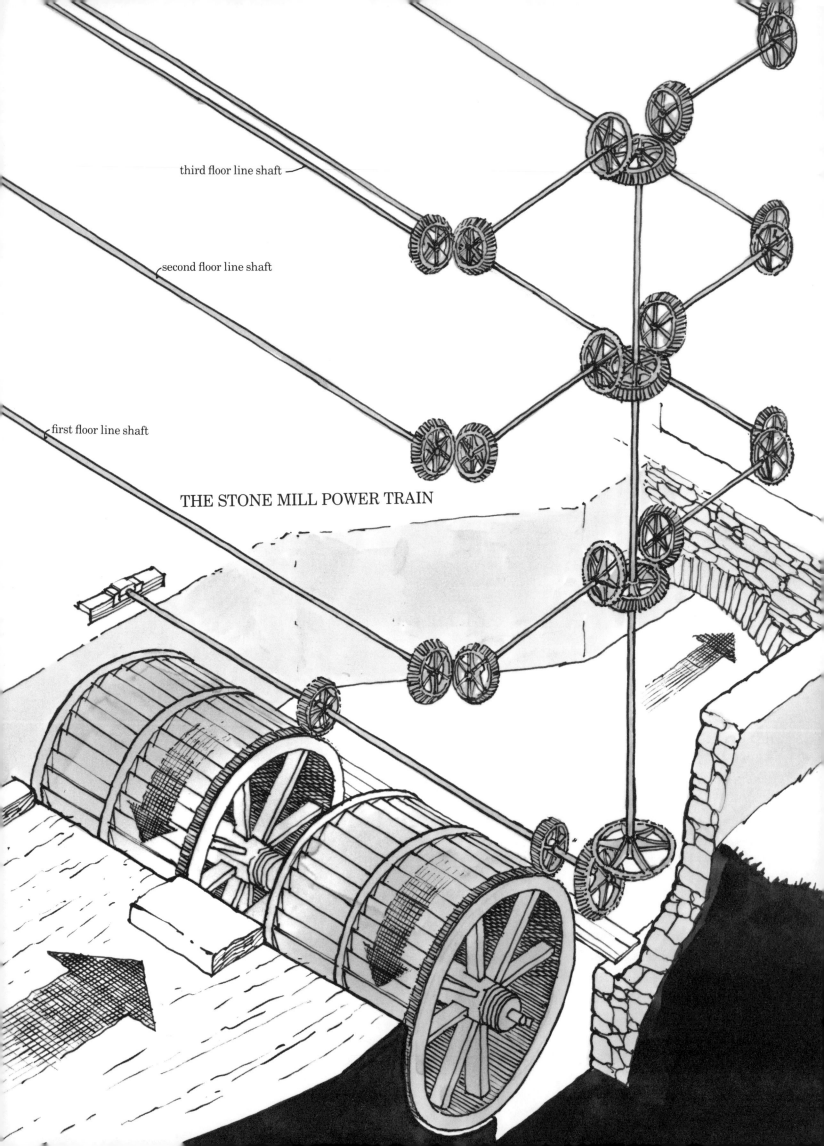

third floor line shaft

second floor line shaft

first floor line shaft

THE STONE MILL POWER TRAIN

A larger mill with more machinery required more power. It was necessary, therefore, to choose a site along the river that would provide a greater head. Plimpton calculated that he could create this head by building a raceway from the falls and extending it to a wheelpit about seven hundred yards downstream. To avoid interfering with the raceway of the grist mill, he proposed to locate the new mill across the river, directly opposite the Yellow Mill. In order to provide adequate flow for the new mill, he purchased the fulling mill and its substantial water rights.

Plimpton planned to create more power for the Stone Mill by installing two wheels. So that the increased head could be used most efficiently, these were to be high breast wheels. Although each wheel would turn in a separate pit, both would be connected to the same vertical shaft of the power train. This time both the shafting and the gears were to be made of cast iron.

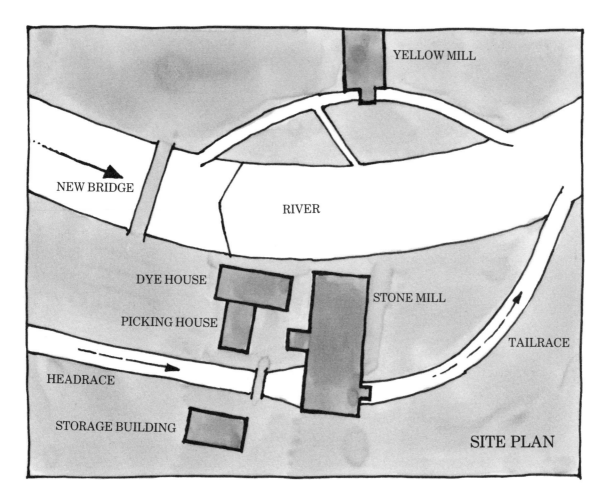

Near the mill, Plimpton planned to construct a number of smaller buildings. The first, to be made of stone, was the picking house. He had decided to remove the picking operation from the new mill because of the tremendous fire hazard caused by the whale oil lamps and the cotton particles and dust that filled the air. He also planned to build a large storage shed and a dye house where the yarn would be dyed before it was woven.

A new wooden bridge was planned that would span the river just above the dam. Until it was completed, the journey from the Yellow Mill to the new site had to be made over the stone bridge and covered almost a mile.

By late March, most of the building materials had arrived at the site. Those items coming from Providence were shipped as far as possible on the Blackstone Canal and hauled the rest of the way by sled or cart. Additional workers arrived in April, and by the end of the month excavation of the tailrace was under way.

By mid-June, the foundation for the mill itself was begun. To withstand the tremendous weight of the walls, Plimpton made this foundation deeper and wider than that of the Yellow Mill. Where the raceway passed under the mill, the building was to be supported by large arches. They consisted of several rows of carefully fitted stones laid over a temporary wooden frame called a centering. The centering was not removed until the mortar between the stones of the arch, and in the wall above and on both sides of it, had set.

As the roughly hewn stones were set in place to create the foundation, Plimpton supervised the absolutely precise construction of the breast wheels and their pits. By the time he was finished, the beams of the first floor were in place.

To reduce the possibility of a major fire and to minimize the damage that even a small fire might cause, he used a relatively new method of floor construction known as slow burning. The main idea was to eliminate as many of the smaller, more combustible pieces as possible and to use larger beams that, even when charred, would still carry a sizable load. Plimpton therefore used very heavy timbers for his main beams and supported each at the center with a thick wooden post. A much thicker floor, built with two layers of planking, allowed him to dispense with joists, which burned rapidly in mill fires.

In laying the floor, he made use of another refinement. A groove was cut along both sides of all the three-inch-thick planks of the first layer. A strip of wood called a spline fitted tightly into the grooves between every pair of planks. This not only eliminated any air movement between the floorboards that might fan a fire, it also prevented oil dripping from one floor to another and made the floor that much stronger.

While the floor was still under construction, the walls continued to rise. Plimpton stepped the inside face of the wall back a few inches at each floor level to provide a ledge for the beams and to reduce the weight of the wall. The walls around the first floor were three feet thick and pierced by a row of rectangular window openings. The window frames were installed almost flush with the exterior surface of the walls, and the sides of each recess inside the building angled to admit as much light as possible. As soon as the wall rose a few feet above the ground, the masons worked from wooden planks supported by a timber scaffolding that was secured to the building through the window openings.

By the end of August, the second-floor beams were in place and attached more securely to the wall by iron rods called tie rods.

During the summer, Plimpton had a number of crevices in the ledge of the waterfall filled to prevent costly leakage. Again, coffer dams were used to divert one section of the river at a time while timber framework called cribbing was wedged into the openings and filled with rock. The entire ledge was then topped with a caplog.

By November, the attic floor was finished, and the carpenters worked furiously to frame and enclose the roof before the first snow. During the winter months, the windows were installed, as were the cast-iron stoves and lengths of stove piping. The interior of the stone wall was then covered with a heavy coat of plaster and whitewashed.

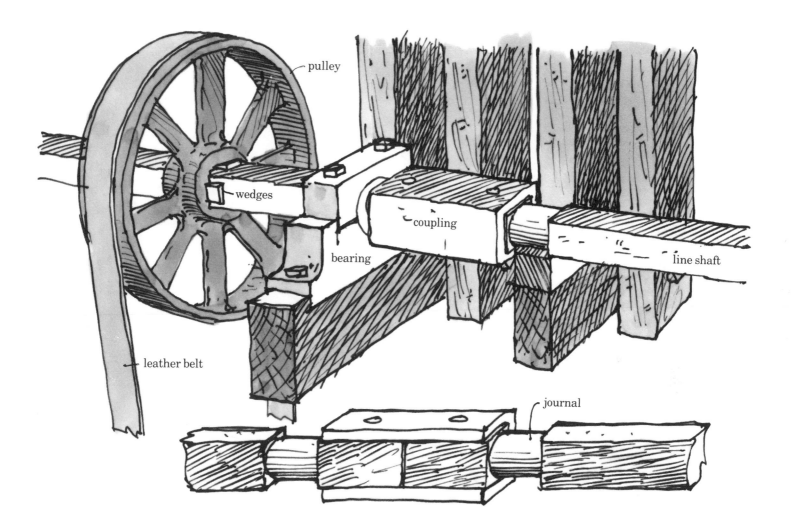

Even before the building was completed, Plimpton installed a machine shop in the basement, where pieces of the power train were prepared for assembly. The shafting was made up of cast-iron sections about ten feet long and two and a half inches square. They were fastened together end to end using square couplings. To allow the shafts to revolve in their bearings, journals were cut near both ends of each section. In addition to continuous drums, a number of cast-iron pulleys were also used on the line shafting.

As soon as the vertical shaft and its gearing were complete, Plimpton installed a mechanism above the wheelpit called a fly ball governor. It was designed to regulate the flow of water to the wheels by automatically raising or lowering the gate, depending on the machinery's demand for power. Without the governor, the water wheels, power train, and all the equipment would speed up if several pieces of equipment were suddenly shut down. Although the change would be fairly slight, it could be enough to break the fragile slivers and rovings.

In April of 1832, the remnants of the abandoned fulling mill were torn down and the headrace extended to the river. A row of heavy timber gates was built across the entrance to the headrace. In front of the gates, Plimpton placed a trash boom. At the opposite end of the headrace, a trashrack and second set of control gates had already been installed.

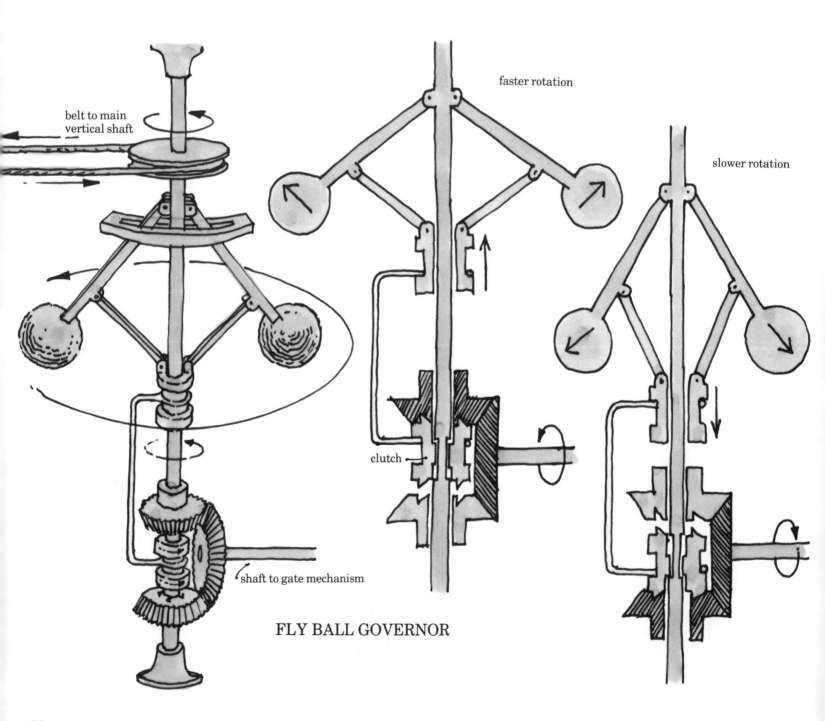

belt to main
vertical shaft

faster rotation

slower rotation

clutch

shaft to gate mechanism

FLY BALL GOVERNOR

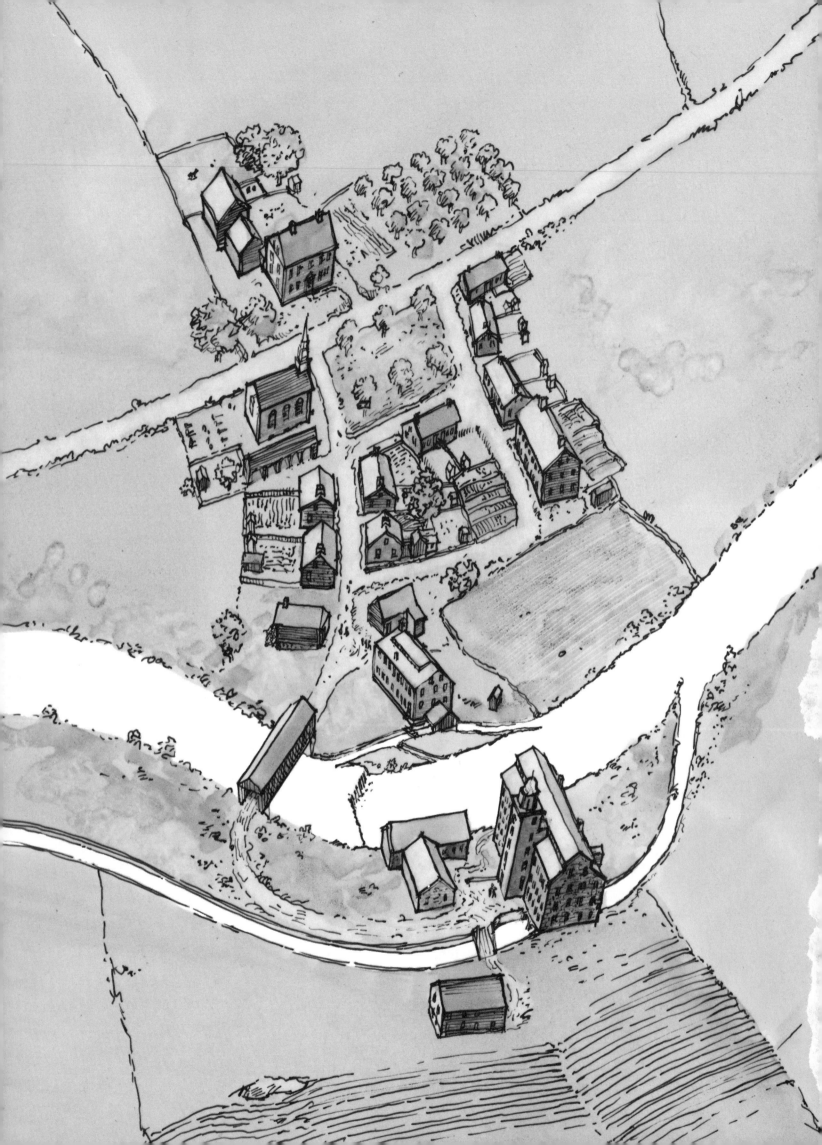

In May, while all the machinery was being set up, the picking house was completed. To reduce the danger of fire, the wooden roof shingles were nailed down over a thin bed of mortar.

Most of the fourteen men, thirty women, and twenty-five children employed by the mill would live either with their families in one of the company's wooden houses or, if they were single, in the boardinghouse. These buildings and a larger company store were all built along a new road laid out between the Yellow Mill and the turnpike, which Plimpton called Company Street.

Once the yarn had been spun, some of it was dressed or treated with a starch solution to strengthen it, and wound onto beams. Each full beam was then secured to the back of a loom. The yarn from a beam would run the length of the fabric and was called the warp. Other yarn was transferred onto smaller bobbins called quills. It would run from side to side across the width of the fabric and was called the weft.

It was on a very warm June day that Plimpton proudly watched the first cloth being woven. No sooner had the weaver shifted the belt from the loose to the fast pulley than alternate warp threads were pulled either up or down by the movement of two wooden frames called harnesses. The space created between the upper and lower warp threads was called the shed. A small wooden container, capped at both ends by a metal point, was slammed through the shed from one side of the loom to the other. It was called the shuttle and carried the quill.

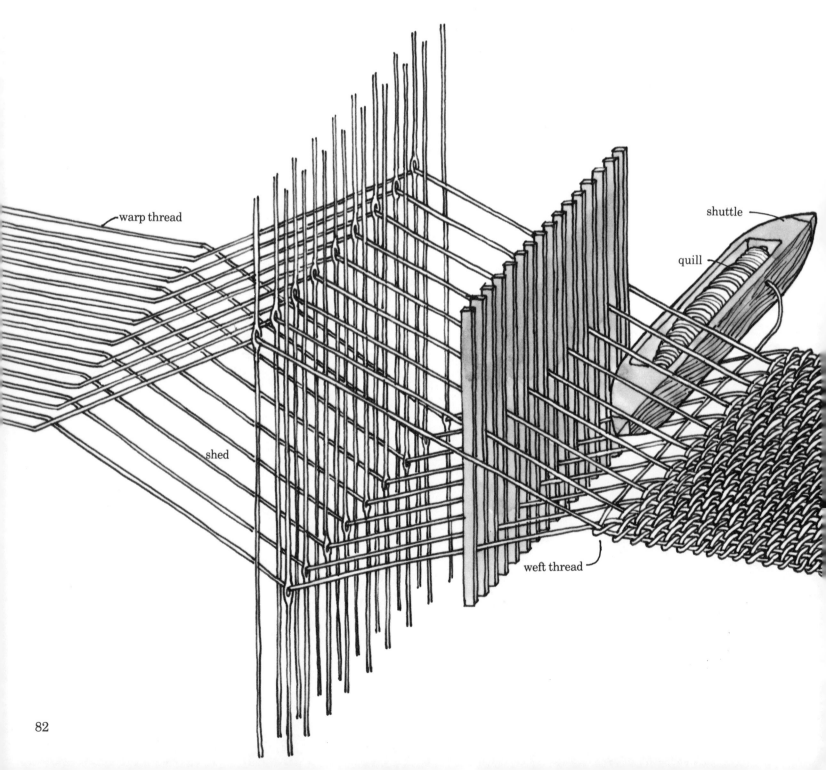

harness

POWER LOOM

When it had cleared the shed, the weft thread left in its wake was automatically pushed into the angle between the upper and lower warp threads. The harnesses then changed position, placing the upper warp threads on the bottom and the lower warp threads on top. The shuttle returned through the new shed, leaving a second length of weft, which was then pushed firmly up against the first.

As this ear-splitting process repeated itself perfectly, inches and soon several feet of brand-new cloth emerged. It was gradually taken up on a second beam located at the front of the loom. Plimpton was delighted by the demonstration and proclaimed the Stone Mill officially in business.

A little of the yarn spun in the mill was sold in the company store, which contained everything from hats and shoes to rice and codfish. Its inventory included such items as ivory combs, wool as well as cotton cloth and yarn, pins, candlesticks, soap, beef, molasses, sugar, butter, seeds, and tobacco. It also sold seasonal items such as potatoes, apples, and watermelons.

In October of 1832, Fanny Adams and her brother Asa came in to buy a spelling book, a writing book, and some quills so they might practice what they were learning at Zachariah Plimpton's most recent undertaking—a Sunday school.

Excerpts from the Diary of Zachariah Plimpton

1833   January   21   Spent two weeks in bed with fever, am now much recovered. Have hired Mr. Ephraim Dodge, twenty-eight years, to oversee daily business of mill. Have high hopes of him ...

Excerpts from the Diary of Ephraim Dodge

1834   June   23   Main shaft broke, bad casting. All hands idle while replacement is cast and turned. Mr. P. informed me today that his son William wishes to enter the mill and learn the business, a most unlikely candidate, I fear...

1835   August   12   No rain for a month, mill stopped for two days for want of water.

            August   15   Ran out of water at noon, sent hands home, cleaned some of the carding machines...

            August   29   Mr. P. and Mr. C. today purchased the saw mill. We can now divert more water for our wheels during dry seasons.

            September   10   Unusually heavy rain for several days. High backwater in wheelpit prevents wheel from turning at speed. What a month!

1836   October   24   Married Miss Mary Plimpton today.

Excerpts of a Letter from Betsey Oliver to Her Brother, an Overseer at the Stone Mill.

Southbridge, Massachusetts   *April 16, 1837*

Dear John,

It seems likely that soon there will no longer be enough work to keep me here. Some of the girls have already decided to go to Lowell, where one of them has a sister presently employed. I think I must quit this place very soon and wish to know if there exists the possibility of work for me in your room. If there is no work in the weaving room, I could learn to operate the spinning machines. If I can be of service, you need only say and I will arrive most speedily. Perhaps you could use more of us ... If there is no work, I think I too shall go to Lowell ... Please let me know as soon as possible.

Excerpts from the Diary of Ephraim Dodge

1837   May   13   Market appears in serious decline, had to lay off several hands today and ask those remaining to tend more machinery. There has been considerable grumbling among the workers.

            May   17   Was awakened at two-thirty this morning by sound of falling bell to discover the Yellow Mill ablaze. Cause of fire uncertain, but was informed that two of the weavers fired last Saturday had been drinking till late at the Eagle. They are nowhere to be found.

            June   2   Mr. P. informed me that money from our insurance claim will be put into new equipment at Stone Mill, market just too uncertain to rebuild Yellow Mill.

            August   17   Took advantage of low water and removed old dam to reduce chance of flooding next spring.

            September   16   Mrs. Dodge gave birth to our son, Nathan, this morning. Fat little face.

1838	April 9	Mr. Samuel Plimpton has taken himself west to seek his fortune. Many tears shed at his departure.
	July 4	All hands out all day, cleaned trashrack in morning.
1839	June 1	Young Mr. William Plimpton married Miss Patience Warren today. Mr. Zachariah P. seems most pleased with his new daughter-in-law.
	September 13	Mr. Samuel P. writes from Texas, all is well.
1840	August 17	Son born to Mr. and Mrs. William P. today, named William also.
	August 20	Our second son born today, named Silas. What a week!
1841	October 28	The Plimptons and ourselves have coincided most joyfully. John P. born this morning, our third son, Jacob, this afternoon. What a day!
	November 30	Mr. and Mrs. Zachariah P. have moved into Providence.
1842	April 1	Mr. Zachariah P. has relinquished his interest in the mill due to his advancing years. Mr. William P. and I have formed a partnership with his blessing.
	April 29	More problems with water wheels, have decided to rebuild them with cast-iron shafts.

Excerpts from the Diary of William Plimpton

1842	May 9	A most tragic accident has robbed me of my partner and brother-in-law, Mr. Ephraim Dodge.
	June 18	Mr. Alonzo Humphrey has agreed to work as agent. He has purchased Ephraim's house, as Mary and the children are gone to Providence.
1843	February 6	My dearest Patience died today in giving birth to a daughter. God has seen fit to take the little girl as well…
1845	September 13	The railroad has come to Wicksbridge. Such an impressive sight steaming across the fields.
1846	November 27	Used up last of sperm oil today, have tapped new thirty-gallon barrel. Lamps are being used about three hours each day.
1847	Thanksgiving	Met the Townsleys today at my parents' home. They are all strongly in favor of abolition, but none brought up the subject of "Negro cloth" except their outspoken albeit eloquent daughter, Rachel.
1849	August 22	Miss Rachel Townsley and I were married today. We will make our residence in Providence, as Mother has been poorly.
1850	March 2	Mother died yesterday. Father seems outwardly calm but sorrows deeply within.

THE PLIMPTON MILL

a self-acting mule

By 1852 William Plimpton was the sole owner of the Stone Mill and a number of other mills in Rhode Island. Having come to share many of his wife's abolitionist views, he decided early that year to abandon the production of "Negro cloth" and to make much finer fabric in a variety of patterns. To accomplish this, he planned to replace the throstles with much faster and more efficient spinning machines called ring frames. They would run about thirteen hundred spindles and produce a strong yarn for the warp. He also intended to use seven self-acting mules. These machines would operate a total of twenty-eight hundred spindles and produce a much finer grade of yarn for the weft. Weaving would be done on a number of new fancy looms.

First, however, William needed to increase the size of the mill. To design an addition, he hired his friend Samuel Belcher, a highly respected engineer in Providence.

After studying the site and determining the requirements of the new space, Belcher suggested a three-story brick extension right off the end of the Stone Mill, matching it in both length and width. Brick, he told William, was not only fashionable and easy to work with, but now, thanks to the railroad, was also easily obtained. He also suggested installing a steam heating system and extending it into the original building. A small boiler house and chimney could be placed discretely behind the addition. Finally, he proposed a new brick tower at the front of the mill. It would be identical in function and similar in proportion to that of the Stone Mill, although updated in architectural style.

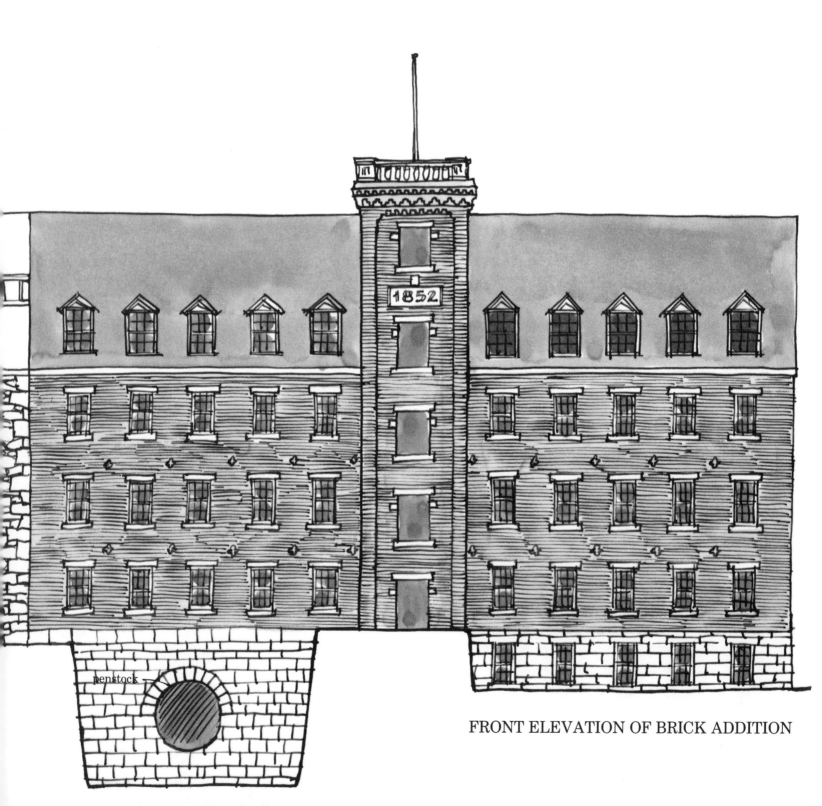

FRONT ELEVATION OF BRICK ADDITION

To produce enough power to run twice as much machinery required a number of major changes in the existing water power system. First and foremost, it was essential to increase the head. This Belcher proposed to do by raising a dam above the falls and digging a new and much longer tailrace. To increase the flow, he also planned to enlarge the headrace. The two breast wheels would be replaced by one more efficient water-powered turbine.

SHAFT

PENSTOCK

shaft

penstock

fixed guides

buckets   wheel

CROSS SECTION

OUTWARD FLOW GATE (moves up and down)

FIXED GUIDES

BUCKETS

WHEEL

WATER POWERED TURBINE

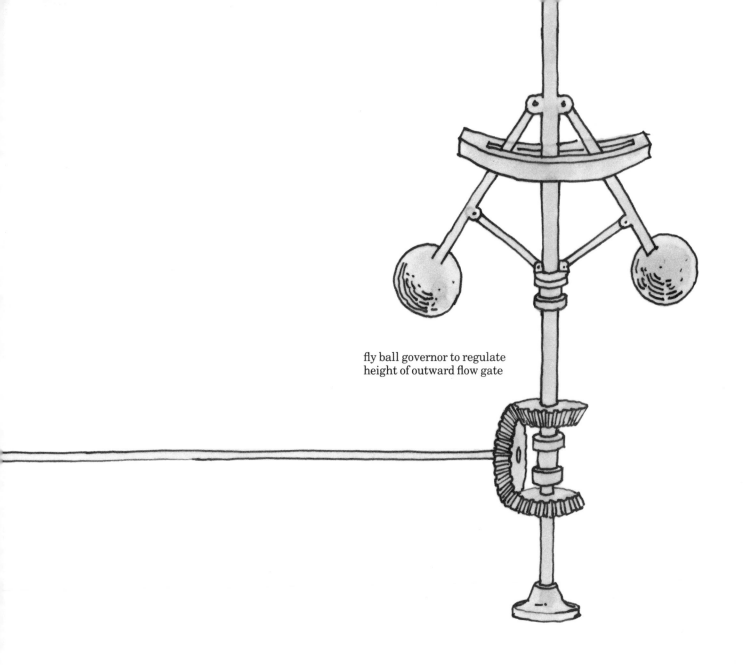

fly ball governor to regulate
height of outward flow gate

The turbine consisted of a horizontal wheel, something like a tub wheel, that turned on a vertical shaft and was placed at the bottom of a large, curved, cylindrical pipe called a penstock. Instead of flat blades, the turbine wheel was equipped with curved iron plates called buckets. A second set of curved iron plates, called guides, was fixed to a stationary form around which the wheel turned. The water from the headrace was directed toward the wheel with a spiraling motion by the penstock. It was forced between the guides, which in turn directed it outward against the buckets. The pressure of the water against the buckets turned the wheel. The water finally flowed out between the buckets and entered the tailrace. A trashrack was installed at the entrance to the penstock, along with a gate that could shut off the flow of water to the turbine. A second gate, inside the turbine, would regulate the outward flow and therefore the power provided. It was automatically controlled by a governor.

No sooner had the plans been approved than materials were ordered and the site prepared. While some laborers dug the tailrace, a second group excavated the turbine pit. It was placed far enough away from the breast wheel pits to allow the wheels to continue providing power for the Stone Mill until the turbine could take over.

The brick walls sat on stone foundations and, like those of the Stone Mill, were stepped back on the inside at each level to help support the floors. When the wall reached the level of the first row of window openings, granite blocks were inserted to act as windowsills. As the wall continued to rise, the wooden window frames were installed. The top of each opening was spanned by a second granite block called a lintel, which supported the weight of the wall above the window.

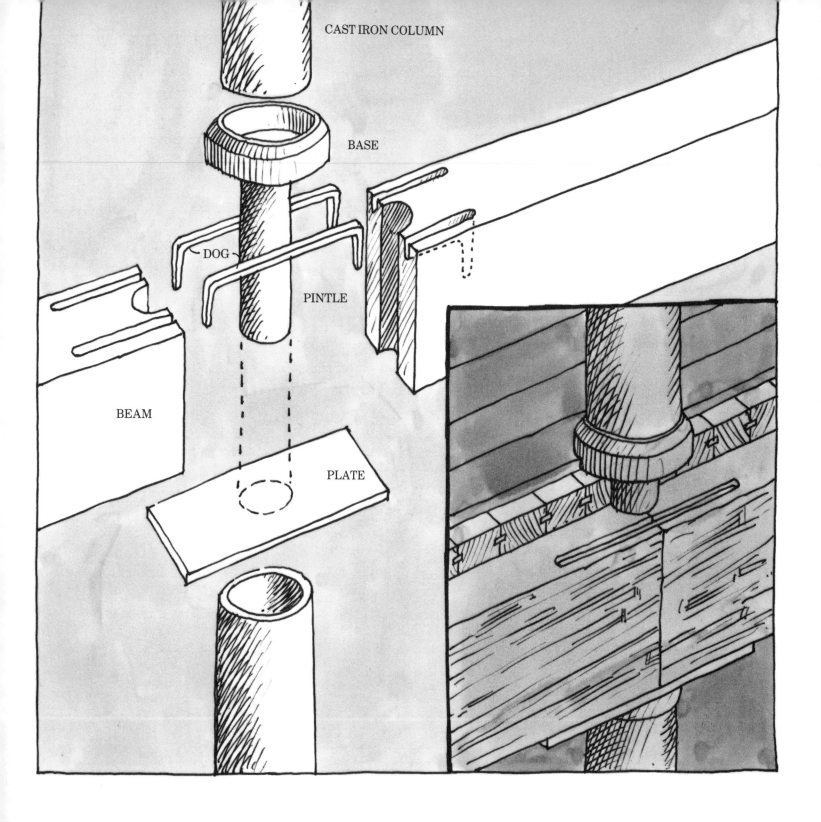

CAST IRON COLUMN

BASE

DOG

PINTLE

BEAM

PLATE

The main beams were tied into the wall as in the Stone Mill, but this time they extended only halfway across the width of the mill. They were supported at the other end by a row of cast-iron columns that ran down the center of the mill. The beams rested on a plate at the top of each column and were tied together by two iron clamps called dogs. Between the ends of the beams and on top of the column sat a cast-iron piece called a pintle, which supported the base of the column above. Without the pintle, the bottom of the cast-iron column could crush the top of the wooden beam and cause uneven settlement in the middle of the floors.

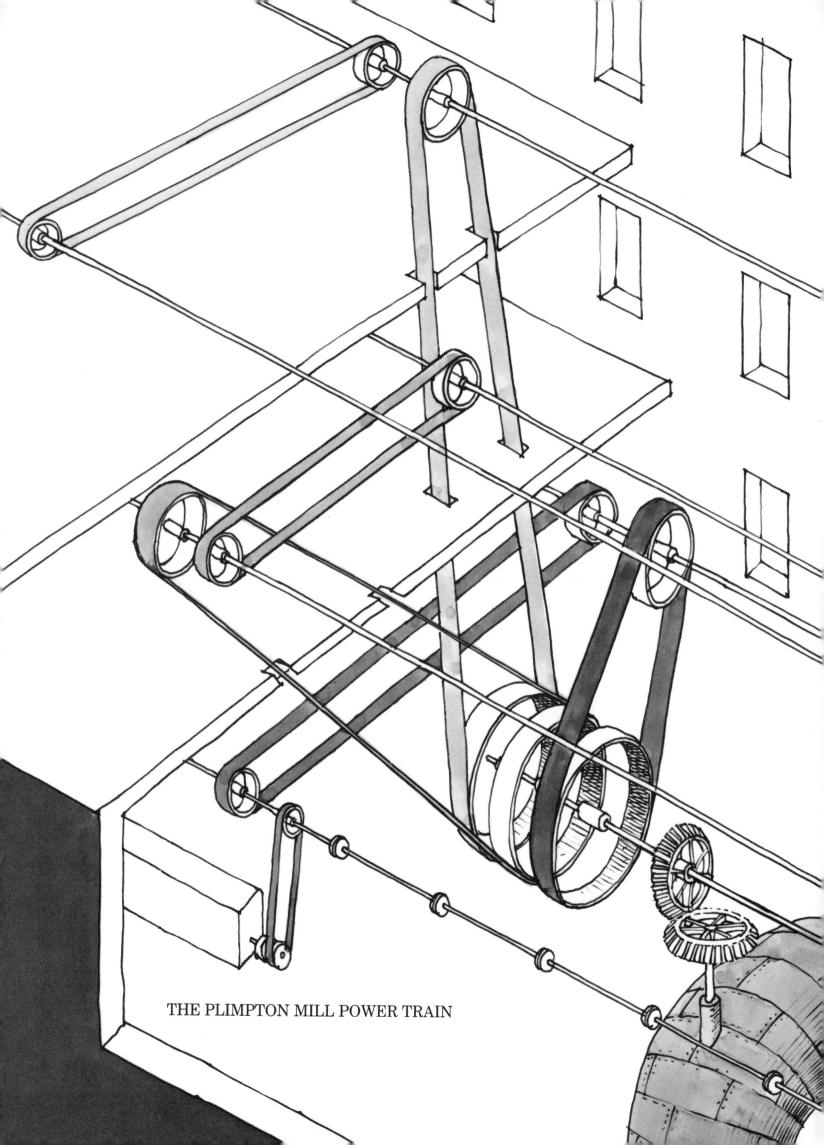

THE PLIMPTON MILL POWER TRAIN

The base stones were set in a channel cut into the ledge and pinned in place. The blocks that formed both faces of the dam were carefully shaped to fit tightly together, while the interior of the structure was formed of rubble and concrete. Soil was banked up against the stone work on the up-stream side of the dam, and wooden planks were driven into the soil to prevent water from leaking through. Both ends of the dam were tied into sturdy stone walls built along the banks. An opening with a gate was built into the base of the dam at one side. This would allow the pond to be drained if necessary. Along the crest, a row of vertical iron rods was inserted to support horizontal planks called flashboards. Although their main purpose was to increase the level of the pond, the rods and flashboards were also designed to give way during a flood. They would have to be replaced almost every summer. A row of new gates protected by a wooden shelter called a gatehouse controlled the entrance to the headrace.

During the summer of 1852 the new dam was built. Its height not only would increase the head but would also assure a constant water supply by creating a mill pond. During the day, the level of the pond would drop as water flowed into the turbine. At night, when the mill was closed, the gate between the pond and the headrace would be shut, allowing the pond to fill again for the next day. To eliminate the last of the nearby competition for water power, Plimpton bought the grist mill and its water rights. And to avoid the legal struggle that would undoubtedly have resulted, he settled an annual payment on two farmers upstream whose land would be flooded by the water behind the new dam.

This dam was to be of the same cross section as the old dam. However, rather than spanning the falls in two straight sections, it would form a continuous gentle arc, and it was to be built of stone instead of wood.

hanger

bearing

coupling

Having overseen the installation of the turbine, Belcher moved next to the power train. To reduce friction and the amount of maintenance, as well as some of the noise, he replaced the cumbersome vertical shafting with a number of wide leather belts. The rotation of the vertical shaft of the turbine was transferred to a horizontal shaft. Leather belts ran from large pulleys on this shaft up through the floors to the various line shafts.

Since leather belts would slip on shafting that turned too slowly, it was necessary to run all the shafting at a higher speed. Belcher therefore removed the cast-iron shafting and outfitted the entire mill with tougher wrought-iron shafting. It was round in cross section, and a disk called a flange was secured to both ends of each ten-foot length. To join two pieces of shafting, the flanges were simply bolted together.

While the power train was under construction, steam heating pipes were hung off the walls and encircled each floor just below the windows.

By August of 1853, the machinery was in place and almost ready to run. The gates at both ends of the headrace were shut, the channel drained and enlarged. A new channel between the headrace and the turbine pit was opened, and the entrance to the now-obsolete wheelpits sealed. Belcher worked with his laborers day and night to accomplish this in the shortest possible time, to minimize the costly interruption of production.

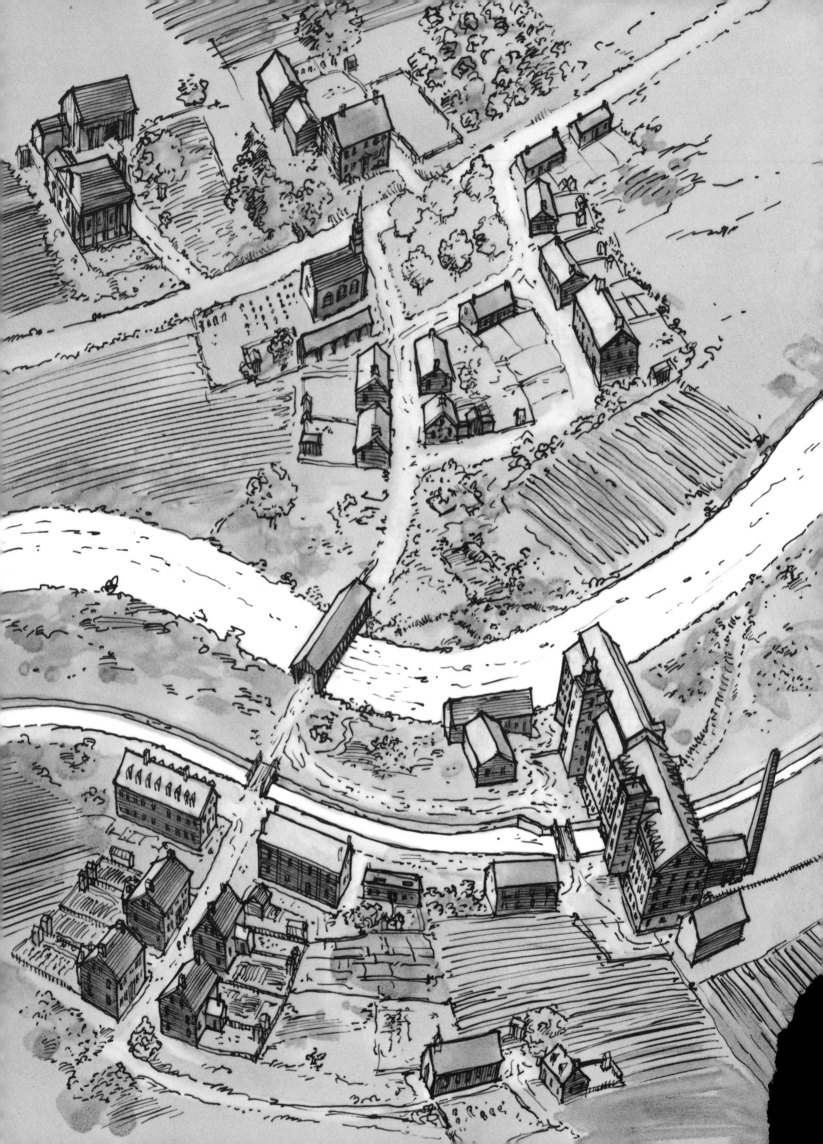

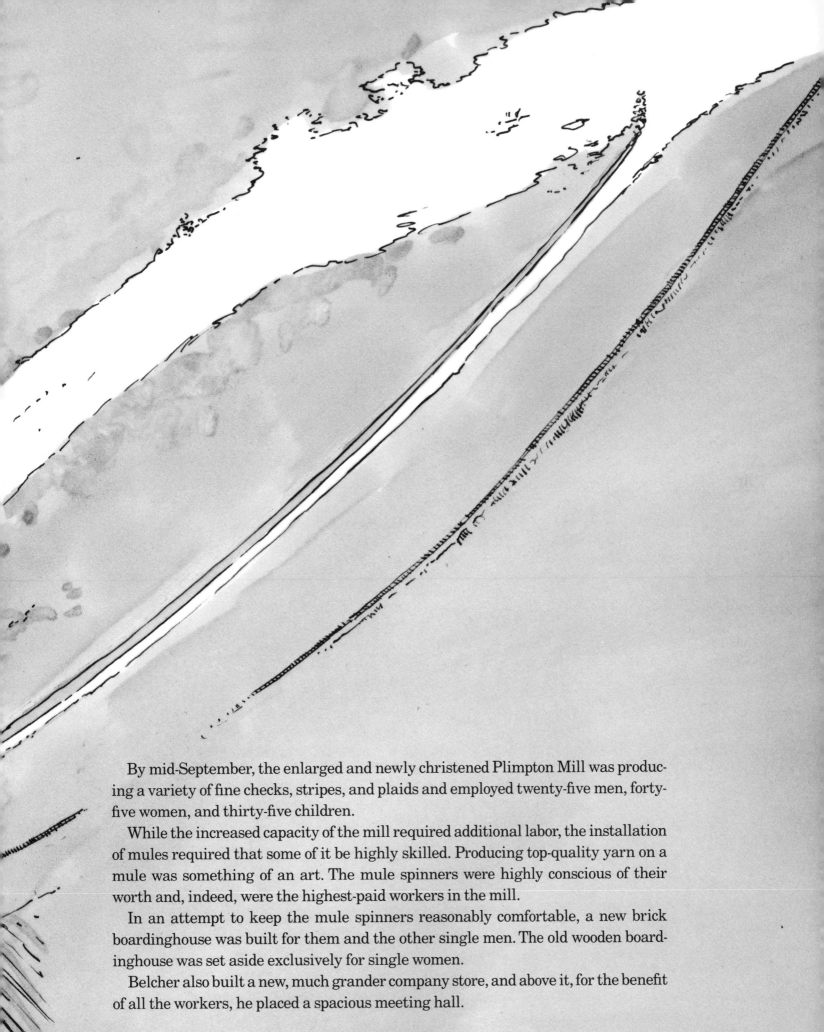

By mid-September, the enlarged and newly christened Plimpton Mill was producing a variety of fine checks, stripes, and plaids and employed twenty-five men, forty-five women, and thirty-five children.

While the increased capacity of the mill required additional labor, the installation of mules required that some of it be highly skilled. Producing top-quality yarn on a mule was something of an art. The mule spinners were highly conscious of their worth and, indeed, were the highest-paid workers in the mill.

In an attempt to keep the mule spinners reasonably comfortable, a new brick boardinghouse was built for them and the other single men. The old wooden boardinghouse was set aside exclusively for single women.

Belcher also built a new, much grander company store, and above it, for the benefit of all the workers, he placed a spacious meeting hall.

One of the first events held in the hall was a lecture by none other than Zachariah Plimpton on the importance of the British contribution to the American textile industry. The fact that so many of the unskilled hands were Irish immigrants probably accounted for the less than enthusiastic response.

Excerpts of a Letter from Dora Sullivan to Her Family in Lawrence, Massachusetts

Wicksbridge   *October 1859*

My dearest Mother and Father,

I hope you are all well. It has been some time since I last received word from you. Father, I am pleased to hear that you, Mary, Ellen, and Bridget find employment at the Pemberton Mill to your liking. I still prefer the smaller mill here in Wicksbridge even though this preference keeps us apart. There are many of our countrymen here, which helps me overcome my loneliness. Widow Kimball runs a good boardinghouse for all the single mill girls. I would prefer a little less boiled ham and more berry pies, but I cannot complain when I think of what we left to come here. Perhaps I will be able to visit you all in a few months. I am hoping to buy a new dress and hat before then.

Excerpts from the Diary of Alonzo Humphrey

1860	January	11	Read in *Gazette* of Pemberton Mill collapse in Lawrence, Massachusetts. 113 dead, 135 wounded.
	April	12	Read today that the Pemberton collapse was caused by poorly constructed cast-iron columns. We put ours in around the same time, tapped them all today. They sound all right, but without removing them it is impossible to be certain.
	September	26	Mr. William P. believes we are in for a long confrontation with the South over the issue of slavery. In case our supply might be impeded and while cotton is favorably priced, we have ordered four times our normal amount. It is to be stored at the Providence warehouse.
1861	April	14	We are at war with the rebels.
	August	8	Jacob Dodge, young William P., and John P. have all joined the Fourth Rhode Island Regiment.
1862	September	18	Heard today Jacob Dodge killed in battle at place called Antietam, William missing, three others from area also killed. John P. is well.
1863	April	4	Belt to spinning room broke today, lost half a day stitching in a splice. One of the girls almost killed by the flying end, but escaped with only a deep cut.
	September	10	Heard of more mill closings today due to lack of cotton. We have been lucky so far in only having to cut production.
1864	August	15	Mary McDonnell was drawn into the machinery by the belting today and lost her right arm below the elbow. I fear the heat will not help her recovery.
	August	17	Mary McDonnell died today, the infection having spread too quickly from her injury. I will send her wages on to her mother in Southbridge.
1865	April	9	Saw John Plimpton today, he is returning to medical school in Boston. Said his brother William has written to him from Texas but that I should say nothing to anyone. Better, I suppose, to believe he was killed in the war...

	April	15	President Lincoln has been assassinated, seems impossible. We are all shaken. Memorial service will be held tomorrow at the church.
1866	March	6	Mr. William P. has authorized me to give land for new Catholic church, over half the hands are Irish now.
	September	19	Read today that Mr. William P.'s brother Samuel killed by Sioux Indians while traveling through Montana.
1867	July	27	Michael O'Brian, Matthew Ryan, Robert Dooley, out half the day, three mules unattended until noon.
	August	16	O'Brian and Ryan out all day after party at the Eagle. Dooley in but useless, sent him home with a warning.
	August	19	O'Brian, Ryan, and Dooley quit today. Will have to go into Providence to find replacements but can't say they'll be missed.
	August	27	No rain since early June, pond drawn down by noon, put girls to cleaning looms and cards.
	August	28	River again low, sent some hands home early.
	August	30	Heavy rain yesterday and all night, all hands in.
1868	April	29	Train derailed, held up shipment of new cotton, pickers idle from 10 A.M.
1869	November	5	Steam pipe burst over looms, lost half a day and fifty yards on four looms.
	December	2	Isaac Skinner slipped into headrace this morning while removing ice from trashrack. He was pinned to rack by force of water entering penstock, was drowned by time gate was closed.
1870	April	15	Heard rumor today that property downriver was bought by the Harwood Company for a new cotton mill. If it's true I hope they build it slowly, our business could be better...

THE HARWOOD MILL

The Harwood Company owned a number of mills and mill villages throughout New England. Most of them had been purchased either from owners who just wanted to get out of the business or at bankruptcy sales. In the spring of 1870, however, the decision was made to build a new and absolutely modern cotton mill. It would contain thirty thousand spindles and seven hundred and fifty looms. All the machinery was to be run by one enormous steam engine.

Designed by Rufus T. Malone, one of the foremost mill engineers of the time, the building was to be of brick, three hundred and seventy feet long and seventy-five feet wide. There would be three floors aboveground, a basement with natural light, and a large attic. All the windows had to be as large as possible to admit light to the center of the wide floors. Two towers projecting from the front of the building would contain stairwells, and two smaller towers at the rear would contain the toilets.

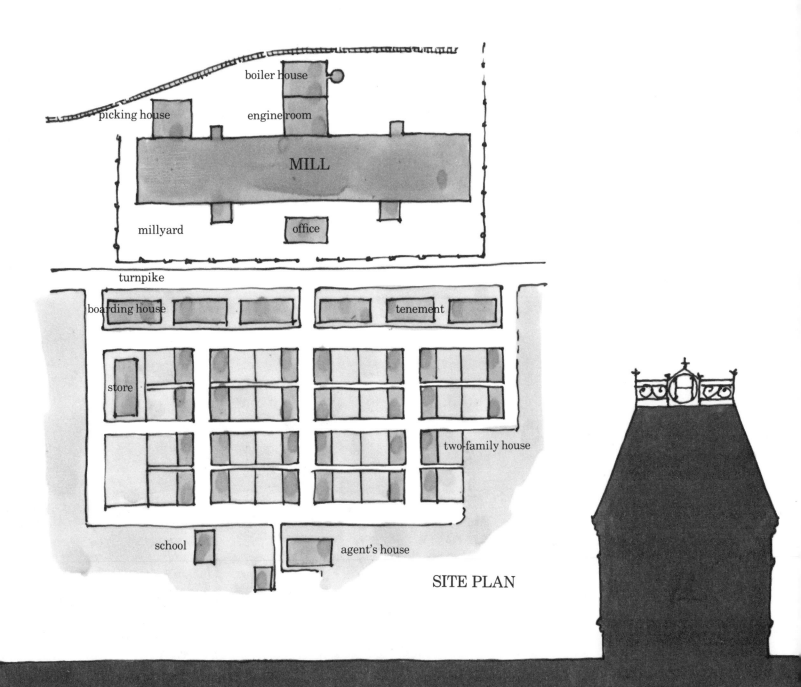

boiler house

picking house

engine room

MILL

millyard

office

turnpike

boarding house

tenement

store

two-family house

school

agent's house

SITE PLAN

Behind the mill, Malone placed the engine house, boiler room, and picking house. The space immediately in front of the mill, called the mill yard, would contain an elaborate company office building and counting house.

In addition to the mill and its outbuildings, Malone's plan called for the initial construction of twenty-six two-family houses with back yards, five tenement or apartment buildings, and a boardinghouse for single workers. These were all laid out on a grid. A large company store with a meeting hall above and a small school were also planned, as was a comfortable house for the resident agent.

A number of sites were studied, but the area across the river from the Plimpton Mill was chosen for its proximity to the railroad, its pleasant rural setting, and its price. A spur off the main rail line was begun immediately to speed the delivery of bricks and other building materials. Eventually it would carry coal to run the steam engine, transport raw cotton, and deliver finished fabric.

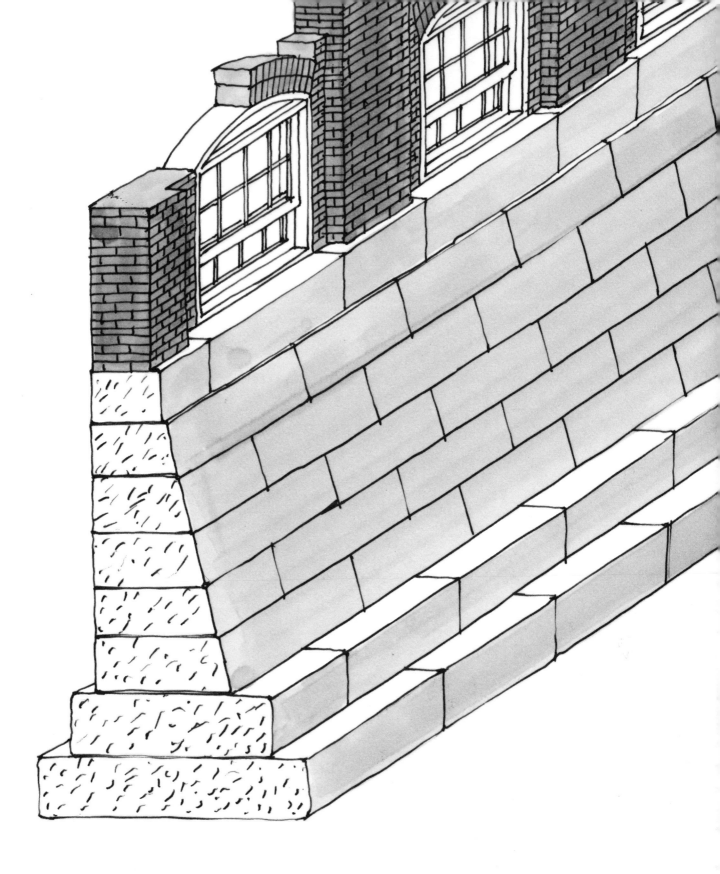

Once the granite foundations were in place, the walls rose fairly quickly. Because of their size, the window openings were spanned by brick arches rather than stone lintels. The wooden window frames were inserted during the construction of the wall, and their tops served as the centerings for the arches. The narrow strips of masonry wall between the windows were enlarged into piers in order not only to support the weight of the floors and machinery but also to withstand the tremendous vibrations.

Running across the mill and connecting the opposite piers were the floor beams. Each seventy-five-foot span was made up of three equal lengths supported at both joints by a round wooden column. Malone had insisted on using wooden columns in all his buildings since the Pemberton tragedy of 1860. Rather than take a chance on large single beams, in which serious flaws in the center could not be detected, Malone built up the required size by bolting two or three smaller beams side by side.

At the insurance company's insistence, the ends of the beams set into the walls were cut obliquely and the openings in the wall made slightly taller than the beams. Although a small metal plate connected the bottom of each beam to the brick, no tie rods were used. Enlarging the openings in the wall and eliminating the tie rods ensured that if there was a fire and the floors collapsed, the walls would remain standing. Malone was not convinced that the walls would be strong enough to be used again after a fire, but replacing the mill would be considerably cheaper if they didn't have to be rebuilt.

The insurance company also insisted that a sprinkler system be installed to extinguish any fire that might break out. A large water tank called a cistern, placed at the top of each tower, would supply water to the rows of perforated pipes that hung from each ceiling.

Also hung from each ceiling were the steam heating pipes. This location had been suggested by the insurance company because of the fire hazard created by workers putting things on or near pipes set below the windows.

Malone took particular delight in the mill's mansard roof. It would be the first in the area and would lend great elegance to the building. The bulk of the roof was slightly pitched, but as it approached the perimeter of the building it dropped abruptly in a steep curve. Dormers containing large windows were inserted along the entire length of this curved face.

flywheel

fly ball governor

crank

connecting rod

cylinder (piston inside)

THE STEAM ENGINE

In April of 1872 the great steam engine was installed. Steam under great pressure was allowed into the cylinder through a set of valves. It pushed the piston inside the cylinder back and forth. A connecting rod and crank transformed this back-and-forth motion into rotary motion, thus turning a gigantic wheel called a flywheel. A wide leather belt on the flywheel turned a main pulley on a horizontal shaft in the mill. Several additional pulleys were placed on this shaft and each was belted to a different line shaft. Once again a fly ball governor assured that the engine met the changing power needs of the mill's operating machinery.

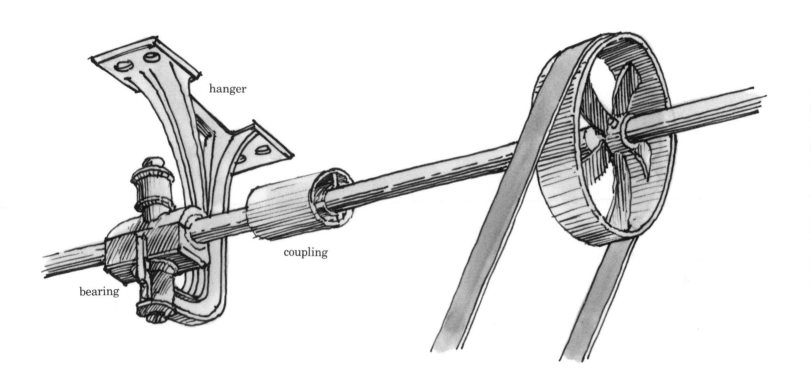

It was almost impossible to keep the shafts from slipping out of their original alignment, because of their great length and because there was bound to be some movement in the building itself. To compensate for this problem, Malone installed self-aligning shafting. It was supported on bearings that were free to move slightly with the movement of the shafting. This not only simplified the installation and alignment of the shafting but also greatly reduced both friction and wear so that the line shafts could turn freely at the desired speed.

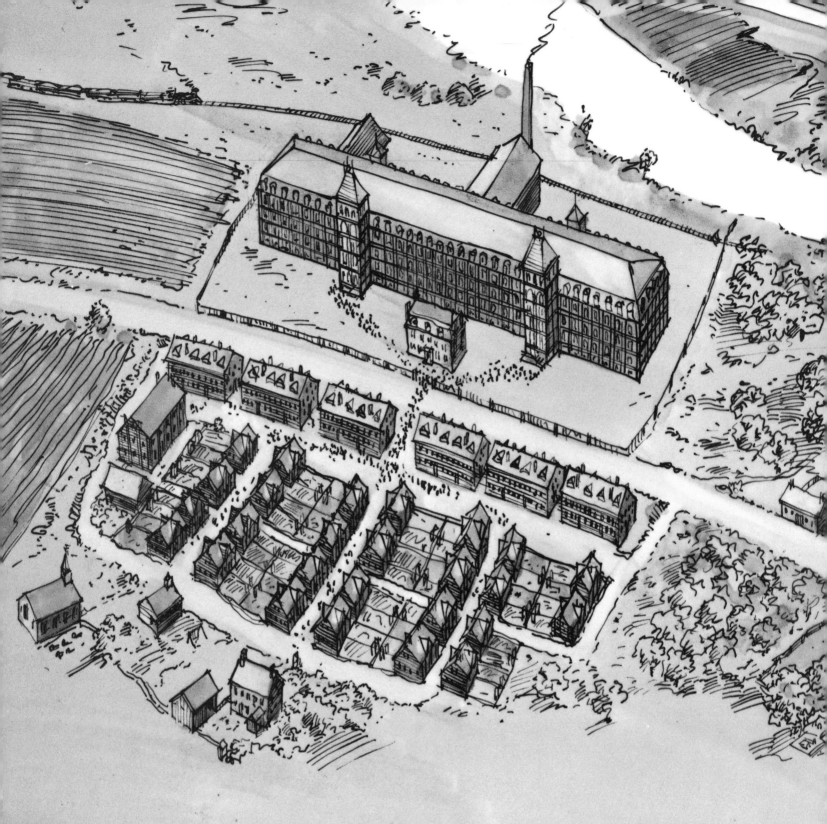

By the end of the summer, the smokestack of the boiler room stood finished, the company offices and counting house had been furnished, and the mill yard enclosed by a high, wrought-iron railing. The gates would open at seven in the morning and close at seven or half-past in the evening, every day except Sundays and holidays. The Harwood Mill began production with a work force of one hundred men, two hundred and forty women, and one hundred and fifty children over the age of twelve.

Across the street from the mill yard, much of the housing was occupied by workers from Quebec. Most of them had been recruited by hiring agents sent to Canada by the Harwood Company.

As the newest immigrants to the area, they could be paid the lowest wages. Before long, a new Catholic church was built on land purchased from the company, and in time the first gravestone appeared in the clearing behind it.

During the preceding seventy years, many sounds had impressed themselves on the area—from the rhythmic slurp of water escaping Zachariah's first wheel and the deafening clatter of the Stone Mill's power looms to the shrill whistle of the first locomotive and the relentless hum of the leather belts. And now the people of Wicksbridge, whether answering the summons of the factory bell or of the church bell, were hurrying through streets that echoed with the sound of French-Canadian voices.

EPILOGUE

Following the Civil War, a gradually intensifying campaign was begun by a number of southern states to attract industry and investment. They offered low taxes or none at all, as well as large numbers of poor people ready to work for low wages without any union protection. By the end of the nineteenth century, these promises, coupled with the opportunity of building new mills containing the latest equipment, had triggered a process that would ultimately squeeze the life out of the northern textile industry.

Thanks to enlightened management, which had insisted on using up-to-date equipment, the Harwood Mill was able not only to compete with growing southern industry but to remain fairly prosperous well into the twentieth century. When the Plimpton Mill burned to the ground in 1893, much of its housing was purchased by the Harwood Company and many of its employees were able to find work across the river.

During the First World War, the Harwood Mill received a number of government contracts. It went on to survive the Great Depression and the strike of 1934 and continued to show a profit right through the Second World War. However, its profits finally declined and eventually disappeared. In 1947, the mill was purchased by B and B Fabrics, which later became a division of the enormous Fabritron Corporation. For the next few years, it was allowed to run at a loss in order to reduce Fabritron's taxes while the firm expanded into a number of non-textile-related businesses in other parts of the country.

As the life of the mill slowly ebbed, the exact opposite was happening all around it. By 1950, Wicksbridge had become a popular residential suburb. Most of the people who lived there had nothing to do with the mill or even noticed it as they drove to work along the highway that now linked the thriving community with Providence.

In 1955, the textile industry finally bid farewell to the place it had created. The remaining operations at the Harwood Mill were suspended, the workers laid off, and the building put up for sale.

Between 1956 and 1968, a number of small businesses moved into various sections of the mill. The last one, a fabric store, closed in the winter of 1969 and moved into a new shopping center. In 1974, the hundred-year-old mill was purchased by a real estate developer who hoped to take advantage of the town's popularity and convert the building into apartments and condominiums.

Workers laying a sewer line below the site of the new parking lot uncovered the foundation of the Yellow Mill and its wheelpit. An archaeological examination was ordered by the Rhode Island Historical Preservation Commission, and much to the dismay of the owner, further construction was suspended for thirty days.

Most of the material removed during the dig consisted of bottles, shoes, and all sorts of refuse. One day, however, a young archaeologist was screening her last bucketload of the day when she came across a most unusual find. There in the bottom of her screen, along with the normal amount of broken glass and pottery, was a corroded but unmistakably identifiable Roman coin.

BACKWATER

Water that backs up into the *tailrace* and *wheelpit* when the river is at a particularly high level.

BEARING

The iron support in which a *journal* turns. Bearings were usually lined with bronze or babbitt metal to reduce friction.

BEVEL GEAR

A wheel whose angled rim is formed with a series of specially shaped teeth designed to mesh with identically shaped teeth on another bevel gear. Two or more bevel gears are used to transfer rotary motion from one direction to another.

BREAST

The curved floor of the *wheelpit* directly below and on the upstream side of a *breast wheel*. It was designed to follow the circumference of that portion of the wheel as closely as possible, to keep the water in the buckets until they had reached the lowest point in their rotation.

BREAST WHEEL

A water wheel whose perimeter is formed by a continuous row of troughs called buckets. Water from the *headrace* enters the buckets on the upstream side (just above the *breast*), and its weight in the buckets turns the wheel. When the water enters the buckets from a point midway up the height of the wheel, the wheel is called a midbreast wheel. If it enters above the midpoint it is called a high breast wheel.

CAPLOG

A heavy timber secured across the top or crest of a dam or natural waterfall to minimize wear.

COFFER DAM

A temporary dam constructed to divert part of a river's flow in order to expose an area of the riverbed.

COUPLINGS

A variety of devices used to fasten the ends of two pieces of either vertical or horizontal shafting together.

FLY BALL GOVERNOR

A device designed to regulate the speed of a water wheel, turbine wheel, or flywheel in order to meet the fluctuating power demands of the machinery.

GEAR

A wheel whose rim is either formed into or covered by projecting teeth. These teeth are designed to mesh with identical teeth on other wheels of the same or a different diameter.

HEADRACE

The section of the *raceway* that carries water from the river or pond to the water wheel or turbine.

JOURNAL

The cylindrical portion of an iron shaft or gudgeon that turns in a *bearing*.

LINE SHAFT

The main horizontal shaft, whose rotary motion is transmitted to a number of machines on a particular floor or section of a floor.

LOOM

The machine on which yarn is woven into fabric.

MILL PRIVILEGE

The right to divert a certain percentage of a river's flow at a given location along the river for the purpose of powering one or more mills.

MULE

A machine capable of producing a variety of weights and strengths of high-quality yarn. It would first draw and spin the yarn, and then in a separate movement wind the thread on its hundreds of *spindles*. A self-acting mule is one in which all these processes are mechanized.

NEGRO CLOTH

A relatively coarse cloth woven in a variety of patterns in both wool and cotton expressly for slaves' clothing.

OVERSHOT WHEEL

A large water wheel the perimeter of which is formed by a continuous row of troughs called buckets. Water from the *headrace* pours over the top of the wheel and into the buckets. The weight of the water in the buckets turns the wheel.

PICKING

The process by which raw cotton is cleaned before spinning. This was first accomplished by beating the cotton with sticks to remove the impurities. Later it was done in a specially designed machine called a picking machine.

POWER TRAIN

A system of *gears*, shafts, pulleys, and belts designed to transmit the power of the water wheel, turbine, or steam engine to the various pieces of machinery.

RACEWAY

The channel that carries water to and from the *wheelpit* or turbine pit.

SPILLWAY

A small channel used to drain the *headrace* for repairs and to carry overflow in times of flooding.

SPINDLE

The earliest spindle was a notched stick around which fibers were spun into thread by hand. Spindles on spinning wheels and spinning machines are the rods that extend through the center of the spools and bobbins around which the thread is wound.

SPINNING

The process by which fibers are drawn and twisted into a continuous thread.

TAILRACE

The section of the *raceway* that carries water from the *wheelpit* or turbine pit back to the river.

THROSTLE

A water- or steam-powered machine with a cast-iron frame and gears that could simultaneously draw, spin, and wind yarn.

TIE ROD

A metal rod used to secure the end of a wooden beam to the masonry wall supporting it.

TRASH BOOM

A log floated across the entrance of a *raceway* to block the passage of floating debris.

TRASHRACK

A screen of closely spaced wood or metal strips designed to permit water to pass between them while preventing the movement of debris into the *wheelpit*.

WARP THREAD

The yarn that runs the length of a piece of fabric.

WEFT THREAD

The yarn that runs back and forth across the width of a piece of fabric.

WHEELPIT

The stone-lined enclosure in which a water wheel turns.